Contents

Contents

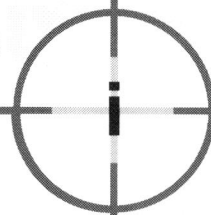

Introduction

The activities offered here are organised according to the examination boards' media concepts so that you can identify them for your planning. The order of the activities does not represent a course outline; they can be selected from, adapted and ordered in whatever way suits your needs and resources. For instance, you may wish to begin to examine generic categorisation with any of the following:

* Film Posters and Magazine Adverts (p.1.6-1.10);
* Film Posters and Magazine Adverts as a discussion exercise to quickly engage pupils in broader considerations of the forms and purposes of genre categorisations, then go on to the film extracts to focus on identifying film conventions (p.1.6-1.10. and p.1.2);
* Genre Categorisations to put science fiction in context and for initial discussion of generic 'crosssover' (p.1.12);
* fruit and vegetables in the How Do We Categorise? activity (p.1.3);
* the Audience and Genre discussion activities (p.5.1-5.3);
* Reading a Film Extract to discuss what we understand about it and why we understand it (p.1.1);
* the Genre and Narrative activity in which pupils 'discover' generic conventions through writing them (p.2.2).

Application of the Activities

As these activities can be used for various purposes, outcomes have not generally been specified; however, there are a few directly outcome-related activities included, such as the essay preparation notes and simulations for practical work. There are also some suggested written and practical coursework outcomes at the end of the Rationale. The activities in the Classroom Resources can be utilised as preparatory tasks producing discussion and structured notes, as parts of a portfolio assignment or as complete assignments. They can be adapted to suit your need; for example, a treatment and/or storyboard an be part of a portfolio written coursework assignment, or part of the pre-production stage for a practical production assignment.

Differentiation

As the GCSE examinations are tiered, the ways that differentiation is accommodated in teaching and learning methods during the course is an issue. The predominant aim here is to work with differentiation by outcome, whilst acknowledging the necessity to provide differentiated support to aid pupil achievement. Where space permits, simplified and extension activities have been included, and these are indicated in the Rationale and on some activities sheets. Overall, it is hoped that the learning focuses in each activity are clear enough for you to adapt the activities to your specific pupils' requirements.

Resources

One of the main challenges for Media Studies teachers is to obtain relevant study and stimulus resources. Examples of print material are provided in this text for immediate use, but they are necessarily limited; not least by size and in colour. There is no substitute for the 'real thing' and some recommended sources are itemised at the end of the book.

RATIONALE

Media Language: Genre

1.1-1.2 READING A FILM EXTRACT

Key Terminology:

It is not necessary to 'teach' terminology at this stage, as the aim is to engage pupils' interest and enthusiasm. However, it can be noted as it arises, then reinforced in later activities.

genre audience audience positioning conventions

Learning Objectives
* To engage pupils' interest and enjoyment.
* For pupils to recognise and value their own knowledge (cultural capital)
* For pupils to make that knowledge explicit and begin to organise and formalise it.

Additional Resources An extract, from a clearly identifiable genre film, of about seven minutes. Opening sequences can be good choices as they introduce the main characters and narrative possibilities. However, a scene with key characters and dramatic tension provides lots of material for the questions – thrillers are particularly useful here.

Notes The questions are deliberately general so that pupils can offer anything they have noticed and to encourage as wide-ranging a discussion as possible. Discussion can be organised by dividing up the questions between groups, then feeding back to the whole class. If you want to make this primarily a discussion activity, the questions have been suitably laid out for an OHP acetate. This activity is primarily designed to be an introductory stimulus to reading films and thinking about genre. It could however be embellished in a number of ways:

Sound Begin by covering up the screen and discuss what meanings are conveyed aurally:
Describe the style of music, how does it make you feel, any noticeable changes during the sequence, what type(s) of film it

make you think of? Describe what noises you hear, what might they be, what might be happening, what effect does silence have? What is said, what type of person is speaking, what is the tone of his/her voice?

Still images: Freeze a few selected frames and discuss what is conveyed visually:

What information do you get about the action?

What information do you get about the character(s)?

How are the elements in the image positioned in relation to each other?

What do the colour, lighting, focus suggest?

Why is the camera here?

Where are we, the audience, in relation to the action?

Sequence of freeze frames: discuss why they have been ordered in that particular way.

Genre: It is often easier to learn what something is by being aware of what it is not.

Offer a selection of genres and, in groups, pupils change this film extract into that of a different genre. It would support active learning if they select, and explicitly identify, what narrative elements they would change, then those elements can be formally identified later as the conventions. Points they should cover include: setting (time and place), types of characters, action, significant objects (iconography), costumes, style of dialogue, visual and sound design.

Conventions

Key Terminology: genre narrative elements conventions

Learning Objectives
* To identify narrative elements.
* To apply narrative elements as a structure to specify the differences between film genres.

Additional Resources Short extracts (c.2-3 minutes of obviously generic films – avoid hints of sub/hybrid genres at this stage). Films are preferable so that sound can be included; however a selection of still photographs can be effective and discussion of sound can be raised.

Notes A preliminary exercise can be a brainstorm to identify genres, which will help to focus the main activity on how you break down those differences by identifying the conventions. There are spaces on the worksheet for only 3 films as, due to the amount of narrative detail to be noted and discussed, doing more can get tedious. It's best to keep this exercise brisk as it is introductory; it forms a basis from which a simplistic understanding of genre as types of stories can progress.

1.3 HOW DO WE CATEGORISE? WHY DO WE CATEGORISE?

Key Terminology: genre

Learning Objectives
* To develop awareness of why it is psychologically useful to divide films into categories or types.
* To develop awareness that films can be generically categorised in a variety of ways, i.e. that division into types of stories is only one way to categorise films.
* Additional Resources Potato, lime, orange, cauliflower, lettuce, apple, green beans, cucumber, tomato, lemon, carrot, grapefruit, peanuts, onion, banana...

Notes This is an idea developed from an activity in the section about 'genre' in *Literacy Terms* published by the English and Media Centre. There are obvious implications for size of class and cost here, though hopefully enough resources will survive uncontaminated for you to have healthy meals after the activities! Items which are popularly mis-categorised, such as tomatoes and cucumbers (fruits not vegetables), peanuts (grow on the ground not on trees); help to focus discussion on the subtleties and complications of grouping. Whilst this can be a stand-alone activity, the learning objectives also have connections with the Exploring Genre activities.

1.4-1.5 GENRE TEXTS AND MEANINGS: CONVENTIONS AND CODES

A Note About the Choice of Terminology
Whilst pupils should use appropriate terminology, it is also desirable for them to engage directly with the texts and explore meanings confidently. Introducing too much terminology at this stage can be off-putting for pupils; it can be reinforced throughout the unit. Awareness of the term codes provides a way to encourage active reading of film texts, and to identify and write about how meanings are conveyed via narrative and technical codes.

Terminology can also be confusing because several different terms from different disciplines (Semiotics, Film Studies, Media Studies) can cover similar ground. For example, a *signifier* (Semiotics) or *image* (Media Studies) is a representation that carries meaning; *iconography* (Film Studies) is another word for image or signifier, but it has more powerful cultural resonances.

You will know which set of terminology is likely to be the most accessible to your pupils. For example, the term *image* provides continuity with deconstruction activities you may have undertaken earlier in the course. The term *iconography* has been used here as its origin is in Film Studies, and it is effective in conveying:
* the generic resonances of particular objects in films;
* the power of particular images, particularly if they become independent cultural references.
Iconography has broad applications: it can refer to iconic stars (e.g. Schwarzenegger as action hero in *Terminator 2:Judgment Day*), iconic characters (e.g. E.T. in *E.T:The Extra-Terrestrial*), and even iconic settings. However, for the sake of simplicity at this stage, iconography has been narrowed down to refer specifically to significant objects.

Key Terminology: conventions image codes iconography context

Learning Objectives
* To remind pupils that all the visual and sound information in media texts carry meanings. To become aware that these meanings are often subconsciously familiar to us through experience of seeing these texts; Media Studies helps us to make our understandings explicit.
* To extend pupils' understanding of audience by hearing different individuals who may interpret the images in a range of ways.

Additional Resources Film stills and posters.

Notes The images are taken out of their contexts for the sake of the exercise, pupils may find the task easier if they think of particular films during both tasks. It is also a reminder that the context does influence connotations.

IDENTIFYING GENRE THROUGH INSTITUTION
1.6-1.10 MARKETING: FILM POSTERS AND MAGAZINE ADVERTS   Activity 1
(various genres)

Key Terminology: characters plot genre stars director budget target audience audience expectations

Learning Objectives
* To identify different types of stories in films.
* To predict possible events and relationships.
* Extension learning: to identify other aspects of film production by which films can be categorised, e.g. stars, budget, target audiences, how audiences know what to expect.
* To consider why films are categorised, e.g. for whose purposes.

Additional Resources Own collection of a range of generic film posters/magazine adverts.

Notes As the main focus here is on generic identification there is less need for pupils to be familiar with the conventions of film poster/magazine advert design. Such knowledge can be concentrated on if you wish to develop this into practical work.

Activity 2 (science fiction sub-genres)

Key terminology: genre sub-genres hybrid genres

Learning Objectives
* To begin questioning the adequacy of broad generic categories to describe films.
* To take an active approach in identifying and naming categories of film.
* To become familiar with the range of science fiction films.

Additional Resources Own collection of science fiction film posters/magazine adverts.

Notes You may wish to undertake this task separately from Task 1.

1.11-1.13 EXPLORING GENRE
Activity 1: Sub-genres

Key Terminology: sub-genres conventions images iconography repetition and variation

Learning Objectives
* To begin questioning the adequacy of broad generic categories to describe films.
* To take an active approach in identifying and naming categories of film.
* To become familiar with the range of science fiction films.
* To consider how interest in a genre and its sub-genres is kept fresh for audiences through repetition and variation of the narrative elements.

Additional Resources Coloured pens

Notes This activity takes a diagnostic approach to learning. The intention is that by 'discovering' the variations within the science fiction film category, pupils will find that they need a term to apply to what they have found. I.e. the term sub-genre, which they can fill in, on the space provided at the top of the worksheet, for future reference.

Activity 2: Hybrid genres

Key Terminology: hybrid genres conventions images

Learning Objectives As for Activity 1. Also:
* to begin identifying specific detail from film texts to provide evidence for points in written tasks.

Additional Resources None.

Notes As for Activity 1.

(Extension) Activity 3: Genre as a cross-media concept

Key Terminology: cross-media concept conventions images spin-offs source

Learning Objectives
* To understand that a genre does not exist in one media form only.
* To understand that generic conventions evolve via a range of media forms that feed into each other.
* To understand that films are rarely stand-alone texts; they are often created from print texts and can themselves be the source of spin-off texts.

Additional Resources Own examples of various science fiction textual forms. TV guides, computers, library.

Notes As for Activity 1. This could also be a homework and/or research activity for pupils to search for texts via television listings guides, the library, the website, retail stores, pupils own possessions, etc. Activity 4 could be substituted for this activity; however Activity (3) is constructed to be simpler and more structured than Activity 4.

Media Language: Genre and Narrative

2.1 SCIENCE FICTION NARRATIVES AND AUDIENCES

Key Terminology: genre sub-genre tag-line audience expectations enigmas plot

Learning Objectives
* How taglines set up narrative enigmas to hook audiences and help them to predict narratives.
* How tag lines convey dramatic conflict, ideas, and position audiences.
* How audiences draw on their prior knowledge to understand these narrative enigmas.

Additional Resources None. However, pupils may like to see any posters you have after the exercise as they often like to check their accuracy – even if that isn't the main point of the activity.

Notes Pupils are likely to remember some of the tag lines; encourage them to choose ones they don't know so that they consider the choice of words more fully. This activity can lead on to discussion about typical science fiction plots; a selection of which is given on p.6.4

The taglines are from the following films, in order: (1) *Apollo 13*, (2) *Alien*, (3) *Aliens*, (4) *eXistenZ*, (5) *Close Encounters of the Third Kind*, (6) *The Day the Earth Stood Still*, (7) *2001: A Space Odyssey*, (8) *Star Wars*, (9) *Men in Black*, (10) *The Truman Show*, (11) *The Terminator*, (12) *Deep Impact*, (13) *Godzilla*, (14) *Jurassic Park*, (15) *Mars Attacks!*, (16) *Stargate*, (17) *Dark City*, (18) *The Matrix*, (19) *Armageddon*, (20) *Independence Day*.

A Note about Narrative Theory
Discussions about narrative take genre into more theoretical territory and may seem challenging for some pupils. However, some level of explicit theoretical understanding is necessary as genre and narrative are inextricably linked. Therefore, these two following exercises provide simplified version of theories: firstly Todorov's about narrative structure; secondly, Propp's about characters as narrative functions. Todorov and Propp were part of the movement of *structuralism*, which has been challenged for not being adequately comprehensive. However, for this stage of learning, structuralism does have some mileage in showing how generic conventions are styles of story-telling.

2.2-2.4 NARRATIVE STRUCTURE AND GENRE PLOTS

Plot Outlines cards

Key Terminology: genre conventions narrative

Learning Objectives

* To understand that narrative is the underlying structure common to any story
* Genre is the surface style in which the narrative is told, i.e. the generic conventions.

Additional Resources None

Notes The pupils write their plots and then read them out to each other; the key moment is when they realise that they have all been writing the same story. It is, therefore, vital to the 'revelation' that the groups have no idea what type of plot each one is writing. Thinking of a plot does take some time in groups, so a time limit and continued monitoring is needed to keep them focused on completion. Time allowing, try to include the additional decisions as they highlight the institutional and film language aspects of genre. Allow enough time for follow up discussion; pupils can identify the differences in generic styles between their versions, and the similarities in narrative events and patterns. Should you wish to incorporate narrative theory into the pupils' work, they can be guided in discussion to consider the stages of their own narratives to identify the three main stages.

(Extension) Activity 1: NARRATIVE STRUCTURE AND GENRE

Key Terminology: equilibrium disturbance resolution new equilibrium

Learning Objectives

* To think about narratives as being put together in a certain way rather than just as a series of events.
* To understand that all narratives have a particular pattern of development.
* To understand that this underlying structure allows for surface (generic) variations.
* To prepare pupils for structuring their own film narratives in the practical work.

Additional Resources None

Notes More able pupils could consider whether or not Todorov's theory adequately encapsulates all narratives.

2.5-2.6 NARRATIVE AND CHARACTER FUNCTION

Key Terminology: character function character types as itemised in the activities sheet

Learning Objectives

* To learn several character types.
* To understand how characters serve as devices to carry the narrative forward.
* To reinforce understanding of narrative traversing genres.
* Extension learning: To examine whether Propp's character types apply to science fiction film characters and adequately explain them, therefore encouraging an analytical approach to theory.

Additional Resources extracts from films for pupils to discuss characters.

Notes This is a reduced version of Propp's original catalogue of 32 characters. The numbering of the extension activities continues from the Narrative Structure and Genre activity (p.2.3) to indicate the integration of character into the narrative process in Propp's theory. The question about magical properties is there partly for pupils to clarify what 'magical' implies, but also to reinforce understanding of the relationship between narrative structure and genre by making a connection between science fiction and fairy stories.

3.1 ESSAY PREPARATION FOR DETAILED ANALYSIS OF SCIENCE FICTION FILMS
Genre Conventions

Key Terminology: genre narrative conventions connotations images mise-en-scéne iconography

Learning Objectives
* To demonstrate knowledge of a range of films.
* Knowledge and understanding about generic conventions.
* To explore how and why conventions are repeated and varied.
* To show how meanings are constructed through the codes and conventions of narrative and film language.

Additional Resources copies of the films studied for pupils to revisit. For the sake of clarity, especially for those pupils with big handwriting!; and to encourage noting details from the film texts, pupils should use one grid for each film.

Notes Examiners like to see a range of films studied as this indicates exploration of genre rather than separate film case studies. It is advisable to study two very different texts; for example in time, market sector, or from different sub-genres; this will help pupils to vary their points. Additional references should be made, for example to extracts which have been studied and, especially, from pupils' own viewing. Making notes about the films under the conventions headings encourages pupils to structure their essays about genre using the films as references, rather than a structure in which each film is written about in turn with its dangers of repetition and lack of explicit theory. Although generic conventions provide the framework, it is essential that pupils give detailed illustrations from the texts to support their points. The activities are designed to encourage recording of such detail.

3.2 IDENTIFYING GENRE

The previous essay concentrates on the identification and discussion of, generic codes and conventions. The essay preparation / writing frame takes a conceptual approach, and may be suitable for more able pupils. It encourages them to explore genre theory in a broader, analytical way.

Representation

Key Terminology for this section: signifies connotation type stereotype representation
More specific terminology is included in the character sections.

Learning Objectives
* To identify typical generic characters.
* To explore the treatment of those types of characters, ranging from stereotypes to complex individuals.
* To be aware of the contexts that influence repetition and variation in the representation of characters, including contemporary culture and institutional issues.

Additional Resources Film extracts (suggestions included below).

Notes The range of conventional characters can each be covered briefly in the language sections. Detailed analysis of all of them is unrealistic and it is generally advisable to support pupils' deeper knowledge and understanding by studying one group of characters in depth. Such an approach also provides a way into understanding representation in terms of ideology, especially the power relationships within which the characters operate.

There are strong reasons for choosing each of the character types here, especially as there have been clear, varied and interesting examples throughout the history of science fiction films. Science fiction has been a good genre for producing more complex representations of **women**, including some strong ones. More typical generic characters, though are the **alien/monster** and the **scientist**. The alien/monster is often a character liked by pupils, and is culturally interesting as it provides metaphors for contemporary fears and values. 'It' also provides a variation of the villain role usually associated with humans. The scientist is a rich generic character, he can be the villain or supporting hero; as well as explaining the science, he also carries cultural values in terms of the moral ideologies and debates central to the narratives.

Pupils should be able to write about three or four characters in detail. Studying whole texts for all of them may be unrealistic for your timetables, extended extracts can also provide adequate information. Below is a selection of suggested case studies comprising a mixture of human, creature and machine. The still images on the resource sheets could be used as deconstruction activities in preparation for, or part of, the main analytical writing.

4.1-4.3 ALIEN/MONSTER

Introductory activity Ask pupils to write down what/who they were scared of when they were little. See if they can identify anything specific about its appearance; what nasty things they might do; sounds; where they thought the creatures lived and why. What did they do to prevent contact, protect themselves? Are they aware of any source for having this particular personal scary creature? The aim of this activity is to begin identifying why the monsters and aliens in science fiction films take particular forms and what the reasons may be, e.g. individual, family, local, cultural myths. The activity will be made much more worthwhile if pupils work in silence and reflect in depth upon what they thought and felt at the time. Similarly, the writing should not be a barrier to expressing their memories, but is important for pupils to find precise words to explicitly identify their fears and rituals. It would be, therefore, be worth preparing differentiated support for the writing.

Suggested examples

Frankenstein's Creature, *Frankenstein* (1931); man-made, grotesque, violent, pitiable;
Invasion of the Body Snatchers (1955); the invisible alien from within;
The Alien, *Alien* (1979); repulsive, malevolent, relentless, seemingly invulnerable;
E.T., *E.T. The Extra-Terrestrial* (1982); benevolent, vulnerable;
T100 and T1000, *Terminator 2: Judgment Day* (1991); man-made hi-tech cyborgs which raise issues about the extent of human control artificial intelligent machines.

The early *Frankenstein* is suggested so that pupils gain some historical perspective, however The Creature in *Mary Shelley's Frankenstein* (1994) may be more accessible for some pupils as the issues related to his suffering are made explicit in the dialogue. The first *Alien* has been suggested as we see the process of its genesis; however the subsequent revelations about it being a mother in *Aliens* (1986) enhance its connotations.

4.4 HERO OR VILLAIN?

The aim of the extension activity is to get pupils thinking more subtly about what constitutes a 'good' and 'bad' character, possibly moving them on to be aware of anti-heroes. The sub-division of heroes is explained in the *Teacher's Guide* and refers to: Tough Guy, Wise Guy, the Innocent, the Outsider, the Noble Hero, as well as any others that pupils might wish to coin.

4.5-4.8 THE SCIENTIST

Dr. Frankenstein, *Frankenstein*; isolated obsessive, bordering on madness;
Dr. Morbius, *Forbidden Planet* (1956); psychologically uncontrolled, destructive villain;
Dr. Steven Falcon, *War Games* (1983); brilliant, cynical, world-weary loner;
Miles Dyson, *Terminator 2:Judgement Day*; black, corporate, family-man.

The historical perspective is a central learning point because of the contemporary scientific developments and the ideological discourses they represent, e.g. Dr, Frankenstein (blasphemy); Dr. Morbius (psychology becoming integrated into popular awareness), Dr. Falcon (nuclear weapons); Miles Dyson (sophisticated artificial intelligence).

Other archetypes and stereotypes of scientists who offer rich discussion include: the mad, evil, genius Rotwang in *Metropolis* (1926); the bookish wimp whose intelligence, professional and moral integrity win the battle and the girl – Dr. Daniel Jackson in *Stargate* (1994); the 'alternative' conservationist and gifted computer communications expert David Levinson in *Independence Day* (1996).

4.9-4.13 WOMEN

There are plenty of stereotypical representations of women based on their sexuality, especially the passive ones of sex object for the male "gaze", and the beautiful virginal victim needing to be rescued. There are, though, more complex representations in strong active roles which, though, are often compromised by elements of reversion to safe stereotypes.

Maria/robot, *Metropolis*; encapsulates the binary opposites of saintly saviour and lascivious disturber of social order
Helen Benson, *The Day the Earth Stood Still* (1951); independent-minded war widow;
Becky, *Invasion of the Body Snatchers*; plucky, steadfast companion to her man, sexually assertive;
Jean, *The Creature From the Black Lagoon* (1956); swim-suited sex object/victim needing rescue from the 'monster';
Ripley, *Aliens*; androgynous-looking commander, fighter; instinctively maternal;
Sarah Connor, *Terminator 2:Judgment Day*; fierce warrior and mother of the future world's saviour.

If you have studied one or two of the suggested 1950s case studies, an additional activity could be to compare representation of the women in contemporary posters with the roles they played in the films.

Audience

General Note

There are two main learning aims in this section on Audience. Firstly to provide a means to fuller conceptual understanding of genre being a tripartite construct of institution, text and audience. Secondly, this focus on audience foregrounds the central issue in practical work made explicit in syllabuses and reminders about which have been repeated in several Chief Examiners' Reports. I.e., that pupils must have a clear target audience identified to inform their creative decisions.

5.1-5.3 CINEMA AUDIENCES AND GENRE

Key Terminology: box office cinema audiences audience pleasures genre audience expectations special FX spectacle family viewing

Learning Objectives
* To become aware of the range of reasons for audiences choosing to watch a film, including genre.
* To understand genre as a construct for audience uses and expectations.
* To differentiate between the reasons for, and the experiences of cinema and video viewing.
* To identify why science fiction films are good cinema experiences.
* To understand that audience pleasures and the popularity of films can be affected by their contemporary historical and cultural context.
* To understand that audiences influence the types of films that get made

Additional Resources Current box office charts (e.g. published monthly in *Empire* magazine)

Notes As well as providing opportunities to develop Speaking and Listening skills, these simple research activities could also form the basis for some classroom research about audience tastes. Pupils, as part of a written coursework or pre-production audience research for practical coursework, can then further develop them.

5.4 ARE YOU A TRUE SCIENCE FICTION FAN?

Key Terminology: fan susceptible The latter word is not 'standard' terminology, but was applied to a section of the audience identified during research findings – see **Notes** *below.*

Learning Objectives
* To identify some audiences pleasures provided by science fiction and films generally.
* To introduce some ideas for pupils' own audience research.
* To introduce the importance of analysing audience research data.
* To show how audiences are constructed into types to inform product design.

Additional Resources None

Notes This can be undertaken as a stand-alone activity, but works more fully as an introduction to the next one: Constructing Science Fiction Narratives for Mass Audiences, especially for the last Learning Objective. The source of the audience information used in these two activities is Michael Barry, Marketing Director of the satellite television channel The Sci-Fi Channel, speaking at a BFI Conference in 1998. His brief at the time was to expand the audience of this niche channel beyond what he called the loyal 'hard-core' science fiction fans who would watch the channel anyway. The institutional issue here was the need to increase revenue by attracting advertisers. Barry's audience research was applied to constructing TV trailers for films and television programmes, but the conclusions and subsequent strategies are also applicable to film narratives.

Follow up activities

Pupils undertake their own audience research, e.g.
* to identify science fiction audiences;
* to identify in more detail their opinions about science fiction films;
* to identify what films they have enjoyed and why.

The English & Media Centre's *Advertising Pack* (1992 pp.58-60) has succinct explanations of quantitative and qualitative research, including the various ways and reasons for profiling audiences. The research can have various outcomes such as being:
* part of a unit on Audience;
* a pre-production activity for pupils' own production coursework.

5.5-5.6 CONSTRUCTING SCIENCE FICTION NARRATIVES FOR MASS AUDIENCES

Key Terminology: hard-core science fiction fan sci-fi susceptible stereotypes mass audience niche audience audience pleasures audience expectations escapism spectacle high emotion point of contact

Learning Objectives

* To understand that film texts are carefully targeted to appeal to particular audiences.
* To understand that careful audience research is part of the pre-production and post-production processes.
* To show how audiences influence the construction of genre and narrative.
* To consider whether the aim for mass appeal affects the nature of a genre.

Additional Resources None necessary. However, a sci-fi convention scene from ***Galaxy Quest*** (1999), for example, could be used as a stimulus.

Notes The Homer Simpson quotation is included as a hint at the stereotypical perception of science fiction fans, and is elaborated in the Problem section. You may wish to do an introductory brainstorm to see if pupils have a pre-conceived notion of a typical science fiction fan though, given that comments can be quite negative and there may be such fans in the classroom, such an activity will require sensitive handling. There are several ways in which this activity can be applied:

* as a stand-alone written task in a portfolio unit;
* as preparation for pupils to construct their own narratives. It may appear that pupils are being encouraged to concentrate on the big budget event film, so it is worth reinforcing the more identifiably science fiction attractions and the smaller budget/independent sector text;
* to constructing trailer narratives by pupils selecting key points from their complete narratives. Additionally, Barry's information in the Solution section about how to make the trailers appeal to a wide audience is particularly useful here.
* This informed pre-production approach should pay dividends in the production process and, thus, encourage detailed and focused analysis in pupils' evaluations.

Institution

This section provides an active exploration of how the concept of Institution plays a role in constructing genre. The production process can be organised to provide generic texts, and the distribution process is the direct link between institution and the audience through marketing and publicity. There is a selection of practical production activities ranging in suitability for 'written' coursework portfolio items (e.g. film poster analysis, storyboard for a trailer), to major practical productions (e.g. film trailer, short film sequence).

Marketing: Advertising, Publicity and Promotions

The SEG Chief Examiner's Report (1999) commented on an overall need for candidates to understand that marketing has different facets, and to make explicit their understanding of them. The four main facets are:

* **Promotions** include premiers and opening night parties, competitions, special deals such as 'double-deckering' (the film and other products being simultaneously promoted, e.g. adverts for Ray Ban sunglasses using a ***Men in Black*** image).

* **Merchandising** is selling products, bearing the film's logo and/or images, which are likely to appeal to the target audience, such as clothes, duvet covers, mouse mats, etc.

* **Advertising** includes trailers for cinemas, television and radio; websites, poster campaigns and magazine adverts.

* **Publicity** includes photographs, reviews, magazine and newspaper articles, interviews for a range of media. Journalists and cinema managers are sent press kits comprising publicity stills, stills from the film, cast and crew credits, and production notes which often include anecdotes, biographies and filmographies of the cast, director and producer.

Although Promotions and Merchandising are part of Marketing, they are not appropriate for Media Studies outcomes; whereas Advertising and Publicity are. Inevitably, there is some cross over – an advert containing double-deckering would be an appropriate outcome, for example. Film Education's ***Film Industry*** pack has useful information.

6.9-6.11 SIMULATIONS

* 1. NORTHERN LIGHTS FILMS / BLUE MOON PRODUCTIONS: Preparing a Pitch and Marketing

Key Terminology: treatment making a pitch getting a deal USP (Unique Selling Point) conventions representation

Learning Objectives
* To reinforce learning about generic conventions and narrative.
* To reinforce learning about how institution and audience are part of generic construction.
* To learn how to present a clear, focused treatment.
* To understand the interrelationship between science fiction narratives and science.
* To understand that science fiction narratives reflect contemporary issues.
* To meet examination aims and objectives for practical productions.

Additional Resources As required from: Making a Pitch (p.6.2), Typical Science Fiction Plots (p. 6.4), Ideas From Science and Society (p.6.5-6.8).

Notes As well as reflecting the structure of the SEG Controlled Test, the simulation format is suitable for WJEC and AQA coursework as it provides a dynamic impetus to teaching and learning methods and quickly engages pupils. You can participate in the role-play as Northern Lights Films' 'representative' to whom they make the pitch; in this way you can monitor their progress, engage in discussion to probe their ideas, and move them on to the next (planning) stage. Alternatively, pupils can pitch their ideas in presentations to each other; they are often constructively honest and helpful in their questioning and comments.

The bullet points in the brief are designed to reinforce conceptual learning, and the choice of small to medium budget range deliberately steers pupils away from relying too heavily on the action and special FX of a big budget product.

This activity has been constructed to be more challenging in two ways. Firstly, through pupils undertaking independent research and writing an original plot. Secondly, although there are several possible outcomes (see Northern Lights Internal Email, p.6.9), it is also geared primarily towards preparation for video work, which demands high levels of planning, independent organisational skills, and a range of technical skills. The marketing simulation for 'Celebizz Inc' is geared primarily towards desk top publishing or drawn designs and, thus, can be used as a simpler, differentiated activity. However, the two simulations can be used as pick'n'mix resources, e.g. to create an original narrative for the 'Celebizz Inc' items; or pupils could use the Moonscape treatment from which to make a video product.

* 2. NORTHERN LIGHTS FILMS / 'CELEBIZZ INC': Storyboard & Poster

Key Terminology: key image   see also terminology on activity sheet

Learning Objectives
* To reinforce learning about generic conventions and narrative.
* To reinforce learning about how institution and audience are part of generic construction.
* To meet examination aims and objectives for practical productions.

Additional Resources Film posters, magazine adverts, storyboard template (p.6.13).

Notes This activity is constructed as a differentiated simpler option. Whilst the tasks can be co-opted into a 'written' unit, they could also constitute a practical unit; however, as the storyboard is a pre-production activity, it needs to have at least one other product submitted as well if it is to be part of production coursework. These tasks might, for some pupils, represent major realistic achievements for stand-alone practical productions, though pupils should be encouraged to produce something more substantial. As film posters are designed to have their information quickly absorbed by a passing public they are usually a simple design, so pupils could produce two or three versions, e.g. targeted at different audiences; a sequence of teaser posters, a film poster and a magazine advert. Making different versions also has the advantage of giving pupils more points to raise and encourages comparative analysis in their evaluations. A video cover has a more complicated design and, therefore, is a strong addition to the poster and storyboard.

6.12 READING A FILM TRAILER OR TITLE SEQUENCE

Another means to gaining knowledge and understanding of conventions, as well as providing key points for productions and evaluations. The main learning objectives in constructing a trailer or title sequence are:
* the importance of selecting key information from the narrative;
* the aim is to tease the audience, not to tell them too much;
* the prime importance of editing, and how continuity editing provides a smooth sequential flow to a fragmented structure;
* controlling variation in pace, especially for trailers in their beginning, middle and end segments.
Pupils tend to try to create complete linear narratives for both forms, so detailed deconstruction of examples, and detailed planning are essential. Film Education and *Empire* magazine have free video cassettes and DVDs of film trailer collections. Otherwise, you can use the trailers from hired videos.

6.13 STORYBOARD

Chief Examiners have commented that the written planning in storyboards is often neglected. By producing little more than comic strips, pupils don't adequately convey the visual and audio technical codes that are part of film narrative construction. The template offers a way to encourage the inclusion of such detail, and can be adapted as appropriate.

6.14-6.20 FILM POSTERS (and magazine adverts)

The activities provide differentiated approaches to identifying and analysing conventions and codes. The 1950s poster activity provides a variation of the practical task, for example to construct and compare one contemporary and one 1950s poster; the analysis should include their institutional contexts, e.g. level of budget, target audiences, sub-genre.

Pupils should be encouraged to take their own photographs, rather than using 'found' images of stars, so they can actively explore visual codes. They can write in their evaluations about constructing a persona to reflect existing stars as a means to discussing character, star persona, and how star personas are part of generic construction. If it is necessary to use found images e.g for backgrounds, historical accuracy or spectacular action, pupils should manipulate them in some way.

Additional Resources Film magazines, such as *Empire*, and entertainment listings magazines, such as *Time Out*. Additionally, local video shops, cinemas and film journalists are sent lots of posters. Some reliable websites with poster images are listed below in the Resources section.

6.12-6.22 VIDEO COVER

This is a preparatory activity to identify video cover conventions. In a simpler differentiated version this could be the main learning objective, whereas detailed analysis is invited in the second and third parts of the activity. The activity as a whole aims to provide ideas for constructing products and key areas for evaluations.

7.1-7.10 CASE STUDIES AND SUGGESTED FOCUSES

The Resources provide means to identify and explore the notion of genre in films; these Case Studies enhance that overall approach through suggesting additional areas upon which to focus analysis. The film texts selected here are a means to illustrate these analytical focuses, rather than being separately itemised as being particularly recommended, although they all provide rich material. The main reasons for providing detailed approaches to studying some texts are:
* To suggest ways of analysing texts through using a central focus which explores media concepts such as institution and representation, as well as media language/ genre, and thus encouraging a broader approach to film texts;
* To develop theoretical discourse through pupils identifying what they perceive to be the attitudes and values (ideology) in film texts;
* To provide some resources for teachers requiring a stimulus from which to develop their own approaches;
* To provide some examples of how pupils can be supported in note-making about films so they have adequate reference detail for analytical writing.

Suggested teaching and learning methods
Rather than specifying final outcomes, the Case Studies provide preparatory note-making and discussion. The speed of transmission and amount of information to be absorbed when reading film texts means that pupils need strong support in recording and remembering their observations. The following are some tactics to scaffold these activities in relation to the way the material is organised in the various Case Studies:
* Divide up the study areas amongst groups who, after consultation, feed back three key points, with textual references, to the rest of the class;
* A variation of the above is to have 'expert' groups for each study area. Each group is then split up into rainbow groups that contain one of each 'expert';
* After an initial viewing pupils decide what they think the interesting issues are and specify what they want to investigate; the areas suggested in the case studies can be used as back-up;
* Organised discussion – e.g. two pairs within groups of four argue a preference for the blockbuster text or the independent text (whether it is more original, real science-fiction, entertaining, convincing, etc.);
* Hot-seating pupils as key characters in the films;
* Hot-seating teacher as a member of the audience or a character in a 'classic' film in order to provide contemporary historical, cultural and political contexts.

E.T.: THE EXTRA-TERRESTRIAL (1982)

This film is a good example of generic repetition and variation and an enjoyable classroom text as it engages pupils of all ages, and both sexes, in quite profound emotional ways. It is therefore useful to consider the film's treatment of the generic conventions of the alien, scientist and technology in terms of how they are shown to invade 'our' familiar worlds of suburbia, home and family. In this way pupils can also discuss representation and ideological values.

TERMINATOR 2: JUDGMENT DAY (1991)

Whilst *T2* has all the pleasurable attractions of an explosive action film; it also offers a discourse about the differences and similarities between human and artificial intelligence, about programmed and learned behaviours. It thus raises conceptual questions such as: are conscious choice and moral awareness prerequisites to what can be considered as truly good and heroic, or bad and villainous behaviour? Or, indeed whether such limited generic typing of heroes and villains helps us to understand this narrative. The log of extracts can also be used for a differentiated approach aiming for character description with illustrative detail and some explicit awareness of their generic narrative role.

The main learning method here is the use of comparisons to analyse representation and to consider values in a dystopian future. It is often easier to reach understanding via this method, rather than just analysing individuals. Another useful pairing to discuss representation is Dr. Silberman and Dyson as institutional scientists; the latter could also be discussed the context of 'the hero'. A comprehensive log of scenes is provided for you to use and select from as appropriate.

As well as the considerations outlined above, other areas of interest that could be more fully explored include:
* The exposition: the various methods by which the audience is informed about the storyline, background information and each character's situation.

With specific regard to T101 (Arnold Schwarzenegger) and T1000 (Robert Patrick):
* Narrative construction through editing (e.g. in the scenes leading up to the two Terminators' meeting in the arcade, a sense of confrontation is created through the intercutting and opposing movements across the screen);
* Manipulation of audience knowledge, expectations and pleasures (Schwarzenegger's Terminator character in the previous *Terminator* film; star persona as a generic indicator, as an icon; technology and special effects);
* In addition to the human versus machine discourse, look at parenting/fathers and sons relationships.

With specific regard to Sarah Connor (Linda Hamilton) and John Connor (Edward Furlong):
* Representation and narrative progress of the changing power dynamics between mother and son;
* Audience pleasures - Sarah Connor/Linda Hamilton as a female icon;
* Additional ideological discourses – motherhood, family groupings, perceptions of 'terrorists'.

AN INSTITUTIONAL COMPARISON OF A BIG-BUDGET BLOCKBUSTER MOVIE AND LOW-BUDGET INDEPENDENT MOVIE:

INDEPENDENCE DAY (1996), TERMINATOR 2: JUDGMENT DAY (1991), DARK STAR (1974), THE BROTHER FROM ANOTHER PLANET (1984)

It is important that pupils on all types of media courses appreciate the significance of institution in shaping genre, though such an approach is particularly suitable for GNVQ. As noted in *The Science Fiction Film: A Teachers Guide* there are many institutional influences on film texts and a context that concentrates only on budget is, therefore, simplistic. It is however a manageable approach for pupils which leads directly to generic analysis, for example the consequent production values and styles of filming.

Further considerations that are manifested in the text could include:
* Relative freedom to express ideas;
* The advantages and disadvantages of the responsibility to attract audiences and repay loans;
* The advantages and disadvantages of working independently or within the full facilities and managers of a studio.

Whilst the popularity of two blockbusters has been proven through box office receipts, the independent films are more unusual for pupils and may seem slow in places. You will know whether it might be preferable to show selected long extracts, though pace is an issue to consider as part of the comparison.

AN EXPLORATION OF IDEOLOGY IN INDEPENDENCE DAY

INDEPENDENCE DAY (1996)

The generic constitution of *ID4* is worth exploring. Serious science fiction intentions are eschewed in favour of entertainment and spectacle and, thus, mass appeal. Nevertheless, it provides a meaty source for ideological exploration; in particular of how strongly traditional values are embedded in the action, relationships and dialogue. These messages can also be discussed in the context of big business responsibilities.

THE DAY THE EARTH STOOD STILL (1951)

With the Second World War and nuclear weapons testing close to people's experiences and memories, the issue of nuclear weapons and America's role in the world were fresh in people's memories. A comparison of such issues, as well as some of the ones suggested in the list for *ID4*, will help pupils to consider the significance, or otherwise, of contemporary cultural, political and cultural contexts on the nature of individual films. Useful sequences include:
* the opening 25 minutes; directly comparisons can be made to the opening sequence in *ID4* with its display of monitoring technology and montage sequences around the world of indigenous peoples and the news announcers;
* Bobby and Klaatu's tour of Washington;
* Klaatu's speech in the closing sequence.

SETTINGS: DYSTOPIAN FUTURES

This approach aims for identification of themes and ideologies through close reading of narrative and mise-en-scène. It foregrounds the exploration of ideas about society as a characteristic of science fiction films. Whilst it is not necessarily good media practice to study extracts out of context, and the choices offered in the Resources may be distant from pupils' cultural experiences and interests, there is a wealth of detail to reward observant and thoughtful reading. Understanding of historical, political and cultural contexts are part of this activity, and pupils could enhance their understanding through research; they should also be able to deduce the various contemporary world views suggested by the texts.

Pupils' engagement could be encouraged by selecting one of the films and playing the role of contemporary citizens compiling written or oral reports to be sent, via a time machine, into the past as a warning.

FOOTNOTE
GALAXY QUEST (2000): 'Spot the Parody' Game

A little light relief can't go amiss, especially amongst such dread dystopian views of the future. The satire in *Galaxy Quest* is predominantly about a television series: *Star Trek*, and about sci-fi fans. However the generic conventions abound, as do issues about narrative constructions and audience pleasures. The parody provides an oblique and hopefully painless way to explore them. If you do not want to include this as coursework, it can be used as a fruitful discussion introduction to the unit.

LES VISITEURS (1993): Cultural Variation

This French film may interest teachers who combine French and Media Studies, as well as those interested in comparing the apparently dominant Hollywood form with a European product. As a fast-paced, time-travel farce, it provides an entertaining cultural generic variation; for French audiences it was the top box-office film of the year, taking twice as much as the second most popular film, *Jurassic Park*. It stars Jean Reno in a more typical French style of acting and character-driven narrative, in contrast to his burgeoning 'American' star persona in Hollywood action movies and science fiction movies such as *Godzilla* (1997).

Suggested Coursework Outcomes

* Essay exploring the repetition and variation of genre in science fiction films using three case studies in different historical contexts. Pupils should select films with clearly differing sub-genres, hybrid genres, historical context, or production values.

* Detailed deconstruction of two extracts from two very different science fiction films.

* Choose two or three science fiction films which had stories and ideas that you enjoyed. Say what you liked about them and give some details from the films.

* Compare different versions of the same film narrative; e.g. **Frankenstein** (1931) and **Mary Shelley's Frankenstein** (1994); **Invasion of the Body Snatchers** (1955), (1978), and **Body Snatchers** (1993).

* Adapt the plot of a Shakespeare play you have studied into a science fiction narrative.

* Choose a scene from a science fiction novel or short story , and write a script and/or storyboard for a film version of it.

* Create a narrative for a new science fiction film. You have been commissioned to produce merchandise for it; create a board game that shows the way the narrative develops. Extra moves forwards and backwards will reflect whether what happens helps the 'good' characters or villains.

* Adapt a science fiction plot you have written into three different media texts, e.g. a comic strip, a poster, a video cover, an advert for an appropriate product.

* What do modern audiences expect from, and enjoy about, modern science fiction films? What might they also enjoy about past science fiction films?

* Market research with analysis of audiences and their preferences.

* What do you find interesting about the aliens and monsters you have studied and the way they are represented in the films?

* Female characters often play significant roles in science fiction films, choose three different ones to analyse their roles in the narrative and how they are represented.

* Compare the hero figures in the films you have studied. Include in your discussion examination of the types of heroes they are, and whether you might classify them as straightforward heroes or anti-heroes.

* In science fiction films, the explanation of the science and the related moral issues, are usually focused on the scientist. Choose three markedly different scientists whom you have found to be interesting; discuss their characters and how the films represent them.

Also see: *Case Studies* and Suggested Focuses *Institution* and *Audiences* sections for practical work

Reading a Film Extract

- ◈ What type of film do you think it is? Why?

- ◈ What do you think is going to happen? Why?

- ◈ What do you notice about the setting?

- ◈ What objects seem to be significant? Why?

- ◈ What type of people do you think the characters are? How do you know? What gives you clues about the relationship(s) between them?

- ◈ How are we, the audience, placed in relation to characters and action on screen?

- ◈ What do you notice about the sound?

- ◈ How does the way the camera is used add to the meaning? What do you notice about where it places you?

- ◈ What do the lighting and colour design add?

- ◈ What else did you find interesting?

1.2

CONVENTIONS

We usually think of genres as being types of stories, or narratives. So, to make identifying different genres more manageable, it helps if we break down the whole narrative into smaller pieces, or *narrative elements*. You will see them listed in the column on the left-hand side below. The different ways in which these *narrative elements* appear in different genres are known as *conventions*. Watch the film extracts, talk in pairs about what you notice about the typical *genre conventions* for each film, and jot down your observations in the chart below.

Narrative Elements	Genre Conventions Film 1	Film 2	Film 3
Film title			
What genre do you think it is?			
Settings			
Time			
Place			
Situations & Action			
Characters & relationships			
Good			
Bad			
Typical dialogue			
Costumes			
Significant Objects (Iconography)			
Film Language (e.g. types of shot, camera movement, lighting, sound)			

1.3

How do we categorise? Why do we categorise?

Activity 1

Sort the items you have been given in the ways described below:

Group them according to their **features** *(appearance, something typical or characteristic)*; i.e. what you notice and/or know about them.

a) Begin by choosing 2 clearly different features, e.g. are they fruit or vegetables? Do they grow above or below ground?

b) Next, see if you can categorise them in more detailed ways.

You might notice features that lend you to dividing the food into several small groups.

Activity 2

Group the items according to their use.

1. Again, choose 2 clearly different categories, e.g. can you eat them raw or cooked; can you eat them as part of a main meal or as a snack? Does the outer 'skin' have to be taken off or not?

2. Can you think of any other ways in which you might use them?

Activity 2

Discuss the following questions:

◆ Why do we categorise a mass of things into particular types of things, how does it help us?

◆ How helpful is it to think of differences between items when you try to understand the features and uses of one particular item?

◆ How might you apply what you have discovered about categorising the food to the way that you think about types of films?

Genre Texts and Meanings

CONVENTIONS AND CODES

Like Morse Code, Deaf Signing, letters representing the sounds we speak, all film conventions are coded meanings. In a film they enrich the text and contribute to developing the themes. Conventions and their codes work in two main ways:

- Firstly the surface meaning (denotation): visual and sound information help us to identify objects, characters and places. E.g., a large metal object, with lots of people on board, travelling through space tells us that it is a spaceship.

- Secondly, we can read broader and deeper meanings into what we see and hear (connotations). E.g., the convention of a spaceship as a form of transport tells us that we are watching a science fiction film. We recognise, and can place, this convention because of our past experience of watching films. Further ideas that the spaceship suggests could be: the technology required to build a spaceship indicates that it has been made by an advanced civilisation; the people on board are skilled and brave; the spaceship and the people on board are vulnerable if something goes wrong such a long way from some sort of base, etc…

CODED MEANINGS: CONNOTATIONS

Activity 1: IDENTIFY THE GENRE CONVENTIONS

Jumbled below are significant objects (iconography) from different film genres. Mark out the ones that you think signify that you are watching a science fiction film:

sheriff's badge   alien creatures   gravestone   time-travel machine   castle
a stage with a chorus of dancing girls   machine guns   cyborg
powerful computers   romantic restaurant   cheeky robot   laser sword
horses   objects that change into other objects or living beings   steam train

1.5

Activity 2: FURTHER IDEAS

You have already identified one connotation of the iconography you have chosen, i.e. that they suggest the science fiction genre. What other ideas do they make you think of? Choose **three** objects from the ones you have marked and note down what connotations they suggest to you. Read the space ship example again to get you started. Remember that *context* can affect the ideas suggested by an object, e.g. a weapon in the hands of the hero is seen differently from when it's in the hands of the villain.

ICONOGRAPHY	CONNOTATIONS
1.	
2.	
3.	

Extension Activity

As suggested above, you can read fuller and more precise meanings in conventions, such as the iconography, when you see and hear them in their contexts; especially in the context of particular films. Choose an object, or anything else you like from a science fiction film you have seen, and say what ideas it suggested to you.

© *Warner Bros. / BFI Stills, Posters & Designs*

© *Twentieth Century Fox / BFI Stills, Posters & Designs*

STEVEN SPIELBERG presents

BACK TO THE FUTURE III

A ROBERT ZEMECKIS film

MICHAEL J. FOX
CHRISTOPHER LLOYD
MARY STEENBURGEN

They've saved
the best trip for last...

But this time they may
have gone too far.

CHRISTOPHER LLOYD "BACK TO THE FUTURE PART III" MARY STEENBURGEN   Thomas F. Wilson and LEA THOMPSON

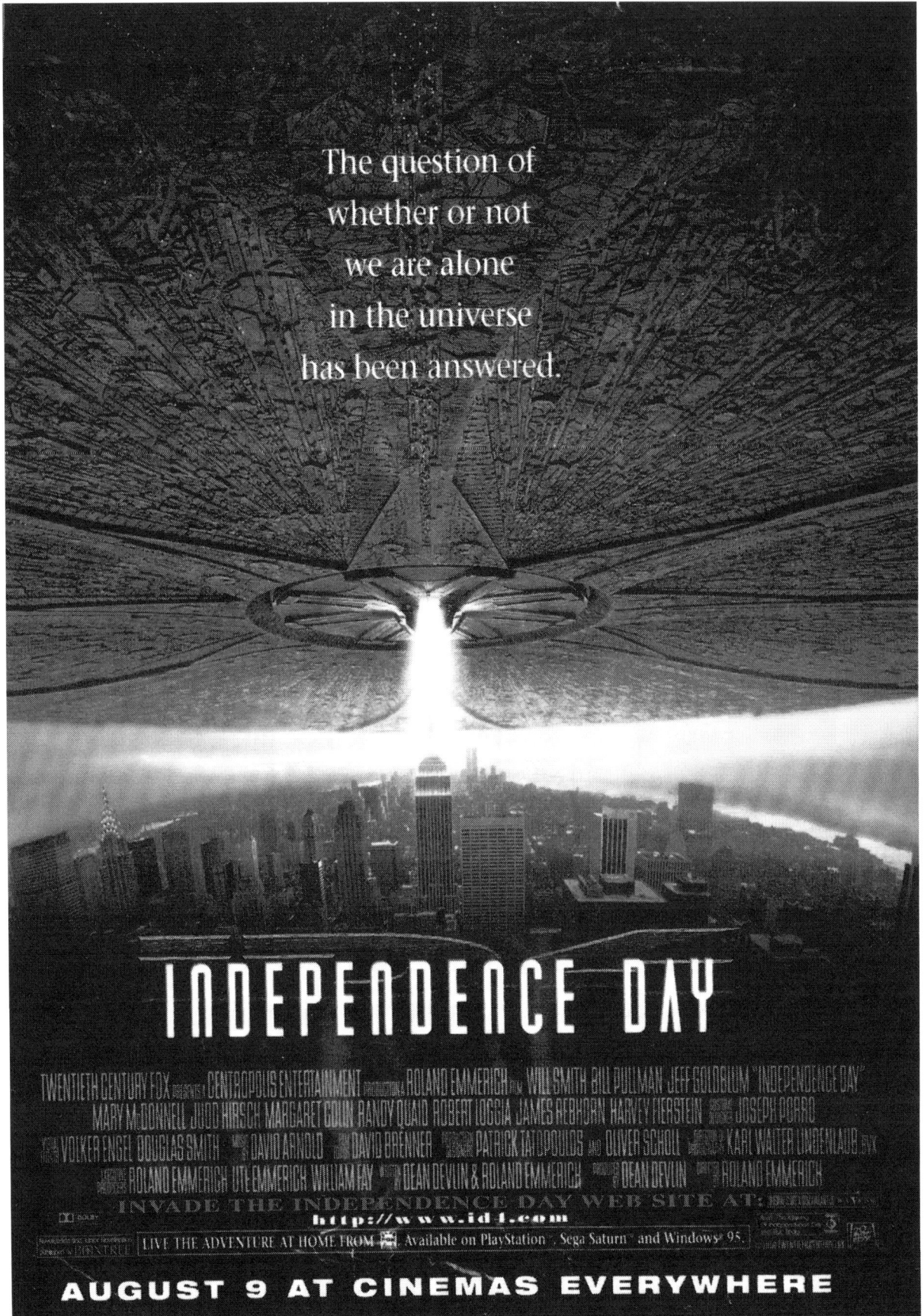

Identifying Genre Through Institution

Marketing: Film Posters and Advertisements

Activity 1

Examine a mixture of film posters and magazine advertisements for films

◆ What information do they give; how do you know what to expect?

◆ Consider stars, possible story/action, budget, anything else…

◆ Do you get a clear idea of the genre; is more than one genre suggested?

◆ How else might you categorise a film other than by the type of story?

Activity 2

Look at a second set of posters and consider:

◆ What type of story do they have in common?

◆ What differences do you notice between them?

◆ What details on the posters make them different?

Activity 3

Discussion questions:

◆ What have you learned about the way films can be categorised through film posters?

◆ What have you learned about the ways in which the science fiction film genre can be categorised through film posters?

Activity 1 ⬭ GENRES

Below are the titles of films that have been described as science fiction films. This assumes that all the films are similar, but is this the case?

◆ Browse through the titles. Mark out with different colours those films which you think have shared features that make them different from the rest of the films.

◆ List each group of films and note what they have in common. Don't worry if you don't know all of the films, discuss the ones you know.

◆ In the space above, write in the terminology that is used to describe such groups of films within a genre. Your teacher will give you the word when you have completed the activity.

THE TERMINATOR

MARS ATTACKS

E.T. THE EXTRA TERRESTRIAL

HOLLOW MAN

GROUNDHOG DAY

2001: A SPACE ODYSSEY

JURASSIC PARK

SUPER MARIO BROTHERS

TEENAGE MUTANT NINJA TURTLES

PLANET OF THE APES

GODZILLA

STARSHIP TROOPERS

BILL AND TED'S EXCELLENT ADVENTURE

TOTAL RECALL

GALAXY QUEST

ARMAGEDDON

BLADE RUNNER

THE FIFTH ELEMENT

INDEPENDENCE DAY

BATMAN

THE X-FILES

THE MATRIX

ROBOCOP

BACK TO THE FUTURE III

ALIEN

THE FLY

HONEY I SHRUNK THE KIDS

MEN IN BLACK

TOTAL RECALL

WAR GAMES

STAR TREK

STARGATE

DEMOLITION MAN

STAR WARS

FRANKENSTEIN

JUDGE DREDD

HIGHLANDER

DR. JEKYLL AND MR. HYDE

JUNIOR

THE TRUMAN SHOW

SUPERMAN

Activity 2 — GENRES

Think about whether any of the films in the complete list could be described as another type of film apart from science fiction.

◆ Select 5 that you know quite well and make notes in the chart below.

◆ Remember to note *why* you think another genre description is also appropriate in the Reasons section for each one.

◆ Do you notice another genre that appears in most, if not all, of them?

◆ In what ways has you understanding of genre changed?

◆ In the space above write in the terminology that is used to describe these different genres within each film. Your teacher will give you the word when you have completed the activity.

Film	Genre		Genre		Genre	
1. Back to the Future III	Science-fiction		Western		Love	
	Reasons	time travel, futuristic car		wild west setting, Indian wars, steam train		Dr Brown & Clara Clayton
2.						
	Reasons					
3.						
	Reasons					
4.						
	Reasons					
5.						
	Reasons					

1.13

Activity 3 GENRE AS ( ) CONCEPT

What else do you know about these films? Are they just film texts?
Do any have their origins in another type of text?

◆ Choose three (or more if you choose) and note down in what
other types of text you've seen or heard them. You could do
some research to find out the origins of the film texts.

◆ What else have you added to your understanding of genre?

◆ How does awareness of the other types of text affect your
understanding of the film? Use the Notes column to jot down
your thoughts.

◆ At the end of the task fill in the appropriate terminology which
describes how the same narrative can be constructed in different
forms. Your teacher will give you the word when you have
completed the activity.

FILM TEXT	OTHER FORM?	OTHER FORM?	NOTES
Men in Black	originally a comic called 'Men in Black'		comic started following reports of people being visited by mysterious men after reporting UFO sightings
1.			
2.			
3.			

What do Tag Lines suggest about a Film's Narrative?

◈ Select about 5 of the film poster tag lines below and discuss with your partner what they suggest to you about the possible narratives, characters and science fiction sub-genre.

◈ Skim over the whole selection and pick out key words and recurring words. What do they suggest to you about the emotions, beliefs and attitudes in the films?

◈ What relationship with the audience is being created?

1. "Houston, we have a problem"

2. In Space No-one Can Hear You Scream

3. There are Some Places in the Universe You Don't Go Alone!

4. Play it. Live it. Kill for it.

5. We Are Not Alone

6. From Out of Space ... A Warning and an Ultimatum!

7. An epic drama of adventure and exploration...taking you half a billion miles from Earth ... further from home than any man in history.
Destination Jupiter.

8. A Long Time Ago in a Galaxy Far, Far Away...

9. Protecting the Earth from the Scum of the Universe.

10. The Story of a Lifetime

11. In the Year of Darkness 2020 ...
the rulers of this planet devised the ultimate plan. They would reshape the Future by changing the Past. The plan required something that felt no pity. No pain. No fear. Something unstoppable. They created ...

12. Oceans Rise. Cities Fall. Hope Survives

13. Size Does Matter

14. An Adventure 65 Million Years in the Making

15. Nice Planet. We'll Take It

16. It Will Take You A Million Light Years From Home

17. Forget the Sun. Forget Time. Forget Your Memories.

18. The Fight for the Future Begins

19. We Hope. They Dare.

10. Teaser campaign of 3 posters for the same film:
EARTH
Take a good look
It may be your last

We've always believed we were not alone
Very soon we'll wish we were

The question of
whether or not
we are alone
in the universe
has been answered

Media Language: Narrative

Plot outline for a HORROR film

Character A has something that Character B needs. It disappears and the story follows how Characters A and B try to get it back. Write a film treatment around this plot using the generic conventions. Also think about locations, sound, music, casting...

Plot outline for a COMEDY film

Character A has something that Character B needs. It disappears and the story follows how Characters A and B try to get it back. Write a film treatment around this plot using the generic conventions. Also think about locations, sound, framing, lighting, casting...

Plot outline for a GANGSTER film

Character A has something that Character B needs. It disappears and the story follows how Characters A and B try to get it back. Write a film treatment around this plot using the generic conventions. Also think about location, casting, sound, framing, lighting...

Plot outline for an ACTION film

Character A has something that Character B needs. It disappears and the story follows how Characters A and B try to get it back. Write a film treatment around this plot using the generic conventions. Also think about locations, sound, casting, framing, lighting...

Media Language: Narrative

Extension Activity 1

Choose two films that you have seen. The films could be different genres, science fiction hybrid-genres, or science-fiction sub-genres. See whether you can fit them into the narrative structure below. *Independence Day* (ID4) has been used as an example to start you off:

Film	Normality (Equilibrium)	Disturbance	Attempt to Solve the Problem	Further Complications	Resolution	Lessons Learned: New Equilibrium
ID4	Various relationships continue as usual	Aliens attack USA cities	Airforce attacks aliens with conventional weapons	Weapons ineffectual; mass deaths and panic; President's wife dies	Nuclear weapons, computer technology, & human heroism destroy aliens	We know there are other beings in the universe. Technology & human ingenuity will protect Earth
1.						
2.						

2.3

2.4

Understanding the Relationship between Genre and Narrative: Todorov

---

THEORY OF NARRATIVE AND GENRE

Genre: the **narrative elements** that change their conventions (their style) in different types story.

Narrative: the way a story is told. All narratives have <u>the same</u> structure and use <u>the same</u> narrative elements: action, characters, setting, etc.

Because the narrative elements and the way the narratives are told are constant, it is possible for the surface genre conventions (style) to change. This is why it is possible to mix genres within a film (hybrid genres), and for genres to both repeat their conventions and vary them (sub-genres). It is the underlying narrative structure that holds everything together.

SUMMARY OF NARRATIVE STRUCTURE THEORY

A Russian, Todorov, proposed that all narratives unfold in the same way. Although there are several stages in the longest section of a narrative – the Disturbance – narrative structure is most easily understood as having 3 broad stages:

Equilibrium: which could also be called normality; the forces of potential conflict are in equal balance.

Disturbance: someone or something upsets the equilibrium and creates a problem. The situation becomes more complicated as the story progresses.

Resolution: the problem is solved and a new, different, equilibrium is established. The new equilibrium is different because life has been changed by what has happened.

Character Functions: Propp

THEORY OF CHARACTER FUNCTION

As we have seen, narrative structures and their narrative elements are constant no matter what the genre of a story is. One of the most important narrative elements is character, and it is possible to identify types of characters that occur in all genres. Propp, a Russian anthropologist interested in myths, spent many years studying folk tales and, after recognising many similarities, proposed the following theory, which has two main points:

- All stories have the same basic eight character types;

- Each of the character types has a role in the narrative, i.e., they add something to the story and take it forward.

Extension Activity 2

Below are the 8 character types suggested by Propp. Looking at a science fiction film of your choice, match the descriptions of the character types to the names of the character types in the lines provided on the following page.

How might you think of "an object with magical property" in relation to science fiction films?

- sends the hero on his quest

- usually by providing a message disrupts the hero's quest usually through false claims

- the main character, who seeks something

- opposes or blocks the hero's quest

- who rewards the hero's efforts

- who aids the hero

- who provides information, or an object which has some magical property

- the reward for the hero and is an object of the villain's scheming

Extension Activity 3

- Do the character types keep the same function throughout the film?

- Do you think the hero means only a completely good person?

- Are there any characters you would change or add?

- What difference to your understanding of the film has this task made?

2.6

Extension Activity 4

Choose a science-fiction film you know and:

◆ see if its characters match the character types

◆ note how they develop the story (narrative function)

DESCRIPTION	FILM CHARACTER	NARRATIVE FUNCTION	Additional Comments
The HERO			
The VILLAIN			
The DONOR			
The DISPATCHER			
The HELPER			
The PRINCESS			
Her FATHER			
Other Character?			
Other Character?			

Genre Conventions: Essay Notes for Analysis of Science Fiction Films

Genre Conventions

Film Title.........................

Setting
Time
Place

Key Action

Characters
Good
Bad

Costumes

Dialogue

Iconography
(Significant Objects)

Film Language
Visual
Sound

Identifying Genre: Essay Notes

Use your notes, details from the films, and the following paragraph and sentence stems to structure your writing if you wish. N.B. They are not necessarily in the order in which you might wish to use them. Discuss your understanding of the media concept of genre gained through your study of science fiction films, and the media concepts of institution and audience.

A genre can be defined as…

Generic categories are difficult to define because…

A film that cuts across generic boundaries is a…

Genre conventions include…

Narrative and genre work together by…

Comparing science fiction with fairy stories is revealing because…

The genre formula offers audiences…

Genre films are important for attracting audiences into cinemas by…

Genre similarity and difference is useful for producers because…

Stars can be important in genre films…

Budgets can be spent differently in genre films; for instance in a science fiction film, rather than paying for big stars, the producers are likely to spend it on…

Typical settings for science fiction films include…

The ideas that science fiction films deal with include…

In science fiction films, threats to society have changed over time…

The visual iconography of science fiction films includes…

Recurrent characters are…

The pleasures of the cinematic experience for science fiction audiences come from…

The Monster, **Frankenstein** (1931)

The Eponymous Monster,
It! The Terror from Beyond Space (1938)

E.T. - The Extra-Terrestrial (1982)

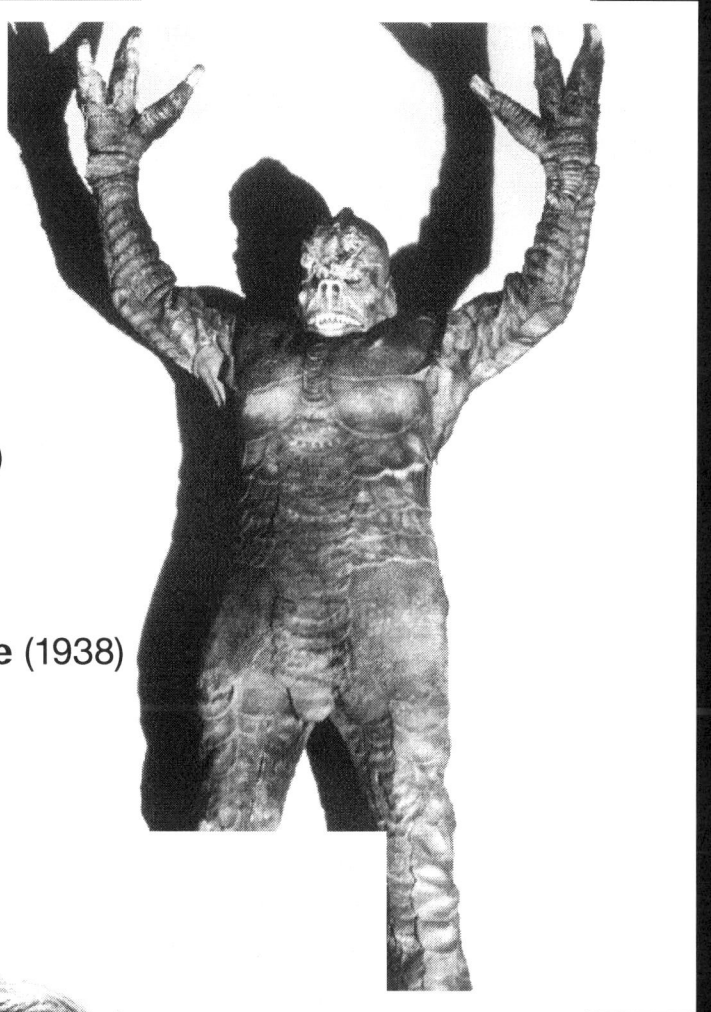

All stills © BFI Stills, Posters & Designs

T101,
The Terminator
(1984)

T1000, **Terminator 2:
Judgment Day**
(1991)

*All stills © BFI Stills,
Posters & Designs*

Investigating Monsters and Aliens

	DENOTATION: what do you see/hear?	CONNOTATION : what does it mean?
Where do you see it?		
What does it do?		
Does it appear to be more or less advanced than humans?		
Is it alone/ masses of them…?		
Do you learn anything about its motives – why it is behaving like this?		
What does it look like?		
What does it sound like?		
Does it try to communicate with humans		
How do the humans react?		
What difference does it make to the humans / to life on Earth?		
Hero or Villain?		

4.4

Hero or Villain

Activity 1

Below are some words and phrases to describe typical villain and hero types of characters. Make two columns, one headed HERO and one headed VILLAIN. Choose ten descriptions for each and write them under the headings.

> brave   truthful   skilled with weapons   merciless
> relentless   has a small group of loyal supporters   destructive
> cruel   awkward with women   has a weak spot   enjoys violence
> has a sense of humour   quick-thinking   attractive   seeks
> power   has abilities that others don't   alone
> gains the love of a good woman   takes the law into his own
> hands   loyal   devious   quick-tempered   immoral
> crafty   reluctant to use violence   seeks justice   devious
> a leader   a protector   exploits others' weaknesses
> doesn't speak   resourceful   physically strong
> has moments of doubt   commands large forces
> a good friend   moral   unattractive   dangerous
> inscrutable   male   persuasive   boyish   a man's man
> a threat to women   pure

Activity 2

Think of the characters you are familiar with from science-fiction films and discuss the following questions:

◆ Which of these characteristics might you put in both columns?

◆ What characteristics listed don't apply to the characters you're thinking of?

◆ What additions would you make?

◆ How might you sub-divide the hero-type, and the villain-type?

◆ What other genre heroes and villains do your science fiction heroes and villains remind you of?

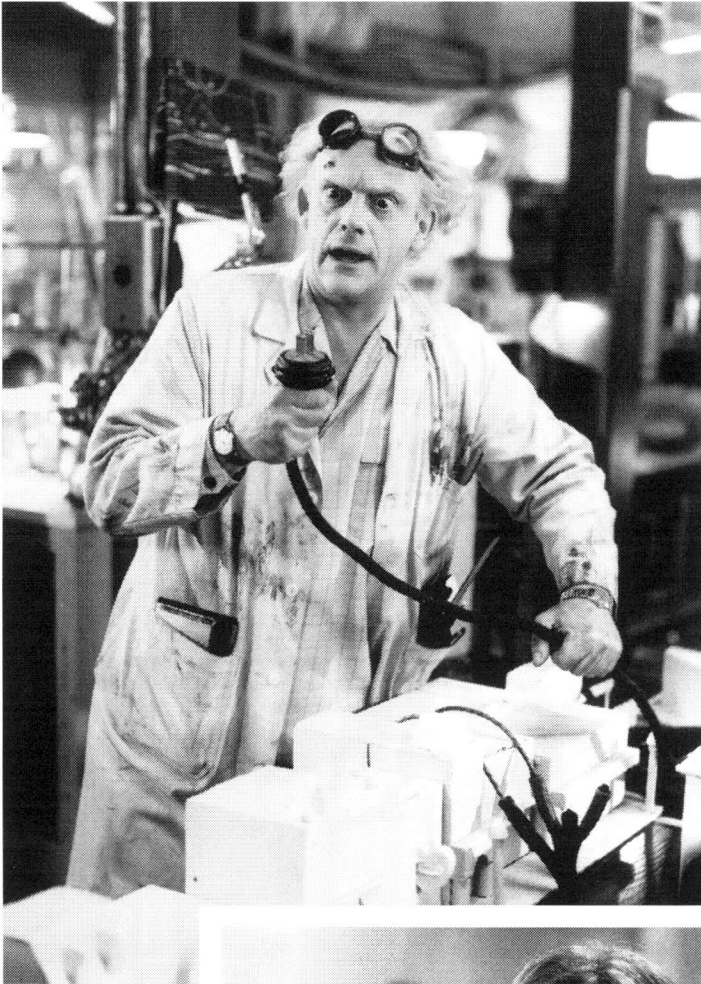

Dr Emmett Brown (Doc),
Back to the Future
(1985)

Dr Daniel Jackson,
Stargate (1994)

l.-r.
Dr Ian Malcolm,
John Hammond,
Dr Ellie Satler,
Dr Alan Grant,
Jurassic Park
(1993)

*All stills © BFI Stills,
Posters & Designs*

© Auteur 2001

Professor Rotwang,
Metropolis
(1926)

Dr Morbius,
**Forbidden
Planet**
(1956)

All stills © BFI Stills, Posters & Designs

Scientists: The Good, the Bad, The Mad and the...

◈ Why is the scientist nearly always male?

◈ Describe his appearance in detail. What is his nationality or race?

◈ What settings do you see him in?

◈ How would you describe the character's personality / the actor's performance?

◈ How is he shown to be different from/similar to the other characters in the scene?

◈ What has he created and why?

◈ What do you think his role in the narrative is?

◈ What ideas/themes is he connected with?

◈ What notions about morality are explored?

◈ Does he discuss the reasons for his actions and the rights and wrongs of them?

◈ What is his attitude to society? Does he reject its values – if so, on what grounds?

◈ What relationships does he have? Are they valued by him?

◈ How would yoy describe a stereotypical scientist? How appropriate is such a description to *this* scientist?

Representation of Scientists in 4 Science-fiction films

Film Title	Character (appearance, personality dialogue, body language)	Setting (where he is, significant objects)	Themes & Ethics (What is his role in the narrative – how are his values shown to be different?)
Frankenstein (1931, dir. James Whale) Dr. Frankenstein			
Forbidden Planet (1956, dir. Fred M. Wilcox) Dr. Morbius			
War Games (1983, dir. John Badham) Dr. Steven Crane			
Terminator 2: Judgment Day (1991, dir. James Cameron) Miles Dyson			

4.8

© *BFI Stills, Posters & Designs*

Jean and the eponymous **Creature from the Black Lagoon** (1956)

4.10

Ripley and Newt, **Aliens** (1986)

Women: The Sex Object, The Companion, The Mother and the...

◈ Does she have a central or secondary role in the narrative?

◈ What is her role in the narrative?

◈ Consider whether, and why, you would describe her as active or passive; does this change during the narrative?

◈ How does she behave in relation to other characters, e.g. the 'monster', the hero?

◈ Give a detailed description of her appearance. What does it tell you about her?

◈ How are female sexuality / masculinisation relevant?

◈ How does she appeal to the audience?

◈ In what ways might the above stereotypes apply to the character?

◈ What themes does she represent?

◈ Is a female 'monster' or villain presented/do we perceive her differently from a male 'monster' or villain?

Additional Activity

If you have studied any of the science fiction films from the 1950s, how accurate is the representation of the women in the film posters compared to their characters in the film narrative?

All posters © BFI Stills, Posters & Designs

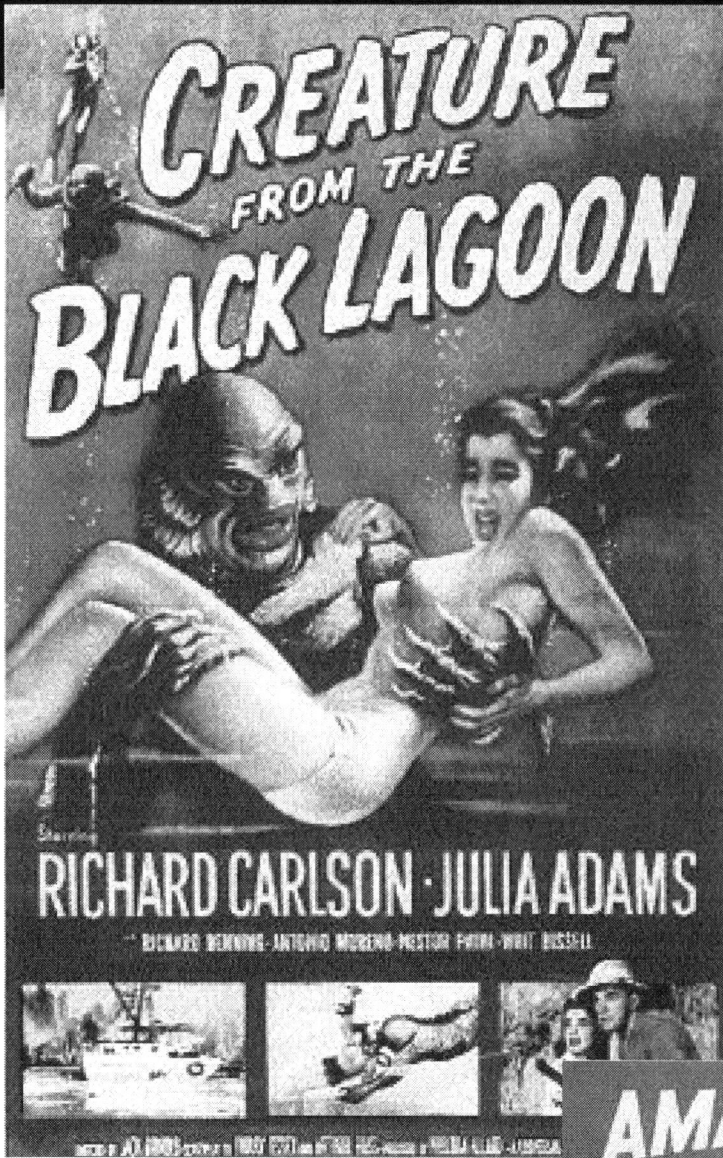

CREATURE FROM THE BLACK LAGOON

RICHARD CARLSON · JULIA ADAMS

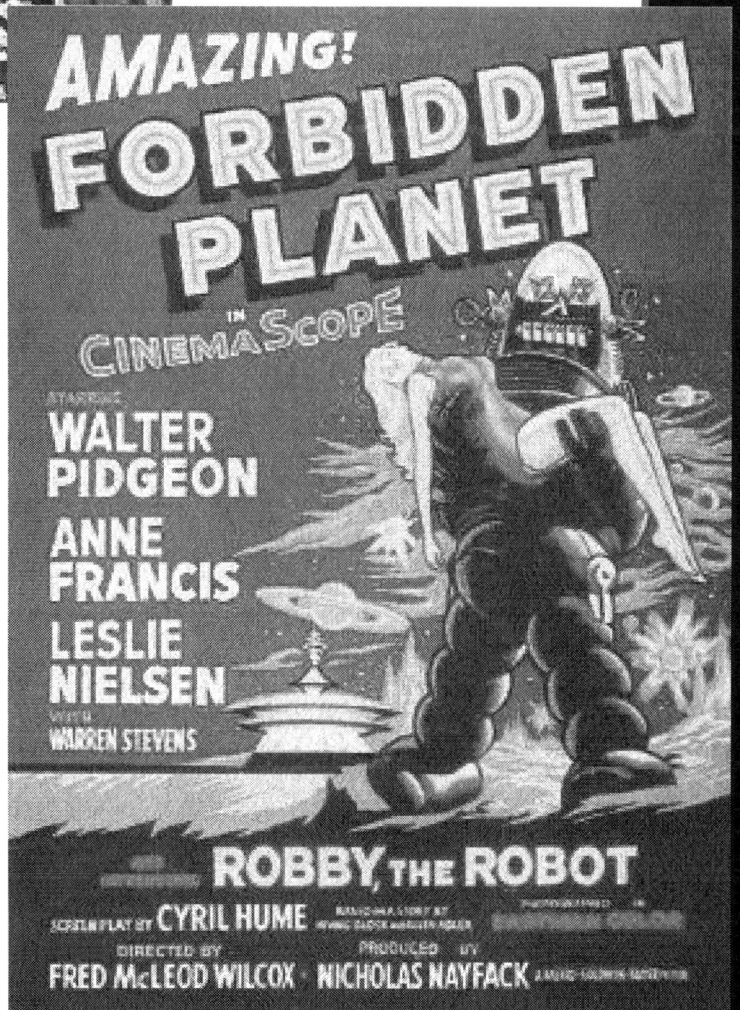

AMAZING! FORBIDDEN PLANET

in CINEMASCOPE

STARRING
WALTER PIDGEON
ANNE FRANCIS
LESLIE NIELSEN
WITH
WARREN STEVENS

ROBBY the ROBOT

SCREENPLAY BY CYRIL HUME

DIRECTED BY
FRED McLEOD WILCOX · NICHOLAS NAYFACK

*All posters © BFI Stills,
Posters & Designs*

Audience

Audience and Genre

Activity 1

Think of, and note down, the last five films that you have seen. These can have been seen at the cinema, on television, on video, or DVD.

What were the reasons for your choices (e.g., you read the review, it was recommended by a friend, you like the star, etc.)?

Activity 2

In pairs look at the sheet with the top films at the cinema box office in the UK and USA for April 2000.

- What types of films seem to have been popular in cinemas recently in Britain?

- What are the differences and similarities to the USA? What do you think the reasons may be?

Look at the list of films that were popular in 1990 for the UK and USA.

- Do you think that, over time, there are changes in what types of films are popular? What might be the reasons? Do any seem to stay popular?

Look at the list of the UK top selling videos to buy for April 2000.

- What do you notice about the most popular types of film bought on video compared to cinema-going? What might explain the differences and similarities?

Activity 3

Look at the list of the biggest overall box office hits to date as of 1998 and discuss the questions beneath the chart (pg. 5.3).

Activity 4   DISCUSSION QUESTIONS

- What and/or who do you think influences the type of films that get made?

- What role does genre play in attracting audiences to films and cinemas?

US BOX OFFICE – March 13 – April 9

	Film	Millions this month	Millions since release	Weeks on release
1	Erin Brockovich	$89.6	$89.6	4
2	Romeo Must Die	$45.8	$45.8	3
3	Mission To Mars	$34.2	$57.0	5
4	Final Destination	$33.8	$33.8	4
5	The Road To El Dorado	$25.1	$25.1	2
6	American Beauty	$22.6	$121.6	30
7	The Skulls	$20.1	$20.1	2
8	My Dog Skip	$16.5	$30.5	13
9	Rules Of Engagement	$15.0	$15.0	3 days
10	The Cider House Rules	$12.8	$54.7	18
11	High Fidelity	$12.7	$12.7	2
12	The Ninth Gate	$11.7	$17.7	5
13	The Whole Nine Yards	$10.5	$56.4	8
14	Price of Glory	$10.3	$10.3	2
15	Here On Earth	$9.5	$9.5	3

▶ UK TOP TEN

TOP SELLING VIDEOS TO BUY
For the month of April

1. **Austin Powers: The Spy Who Shagged Me**
   £15.99, Entertainment
2. **American Pie**
   £15.99, CIC
3. **South Park: Bigger, Longer and Uncut**
   £14.99, Warner
4. **The Indiana Jones Trilogy**
   £34.99, CIC
5. **The Aristocats**
   £14.99, Walt Disney
6. **The Fox And The Hound**
   £14.99, Walt Disney
7. **The Jungle Book**
   £16.99, Walt Disney
8. **The Mummy**
   £14.99, Universal
9. **Pinocchio**
   £14.99, Walt Disney
9. **Pocahontas 2**
   £14.99, Walt Disney

▶ 10 YEARS AGO...

UK Box Office: Top 10
For the month of June 1990

1. Look Who's Talking
2. The War Of The Roses
3. Tango and Cash
4. The Hunt For Red October
5. Uncle Buck
6. All Dogs Go To Heaven
7. Always
8. The Rescuers
9. Honey I Shrunk The Kids
10. Driving Miss Daisey

▶ 10 YEARS AGO...

US Box Office: Top 10
For the month of June 1990

1. Teenage Mutant Ninja Turtles
2. Pretty Woman
3. The Hunt For Red October
4. Ernest Goes To Jail
5. The First Power
6. Driving Miss Daisey
7. I Love You To Death
8. Crazy People
9. Cry Baby
10. Opportunity Knocks

Source: Screen International

UK BOX OFFICE March 13 – April 9

	Film	Millions this month	Millions since release	Weeks on release
1	American Beauty	£4.5	£18.8	11
2	Toy Story 2	£3.5	£42.2	10
3	The Green Mile	£3.2	£6.1	7
4	Three Kings	£2.8	£5.8	6
5	The Talented Mr. Ripley	£2.2	£6.4	7
6	Lake Placid	£2.0	£2.0	2
7	Erin Brockovich	£1.6	£1.6	3 days
8	The Beach	£1.3	£12.9	9
9	Being John Malkovich	£1.3	£1.3	4
10	A Clockwork Orange	£1.3	£1.3	4
11	The Cider House Rules	£1.0	£1.0	4
12	Magnolia	£1.0	£1.0	4
13	The Insider	£0.9	£1.3	5
14	Any Given Sunday	£0.7	£0.7	2
15	The Miracle Maker	£0.3	£0.3	2

5.3

THE TOP 10 BIGGEST BOX OFFICE HITS
(as at NOVEMBER 1998)

1 TITANIC (1997)

2 STAR WARS (1977)

3 E.T.: THE EXTRA TERRESTRIAL (1982)

4 JURASSIC PARK (1993)

5 FORREST GUMP (1994)

6 THE LION KING (1994)

7 THE RETURN OF THE JEDI (1983)

8 INDEPENDENCE DAY (1996)

9 THE EMPIRE STRIKES BACK (1980)

10 HOME ALONE (1990)

✦ Why do you think these films have such broad appeal?

✦ How many of these top ten films seen at the cinema are science fiction?

✦ Why do you think science fiction films are so popular at the cinema?

✦ How many science fiction films can you think of that have been released recently?

✦ Why do you think that science fiction films were so popular at this time?

Are you a true Science-Fiction fan??

Forget J17, this is the personality quiz that really matters.

Find out whether you've got universal appeal or whether you're two stars short of a galaxy.

Select one answer for each of the following questions:

1 Do you really like:
  a Fantasy
  b Reality
  c A nice cup of tea

2 Do you prefer:
  a The unbelievable
  b The believable
  c The blindingly obvious

3 Are you stimulated by:
  a Intellectual challenge
  b Emotional involvement
  c Eating doughnuts

4 Do you like settings which are:
  a Space-based
  b Earth-bound
  c Belgium

5 Do you enjoy:
  a Brilliant Technology
  b An emotionally gripping story
  c Nice wallpaper

6 Are you thrilled by:
  a Action and special FX
  b Interesting characters and relationships
  c Smart shoes

7 Would you rather meet:
  a Captain Jane Rodway
  b Princess Leia
  c Denise Van Outen

If you have answered mostly 'a', then you are a true science fiction fan.
If you have answered mostly 'b', then you are a science fiction susceptible
If you have answered mostly 'c'; are you an alien desperately trying to pretend you're a human?

Constructing Science Fiction Narratives for Mass Audiences

"This can't be a sci-fi convention, it's full of nerds."
Homer Simpson

Problems

When it was doing audience research to find out how to expand its audience, the *Sci-Fi Channel* identified two main problems:

- Science fiction has a steady, but small (niche) audience; films have to appeal to mass audiences to make big profits;
- Most people said they didn't like science fiction films because they associated them with geeky technology freaks, who are a bit intellectual and generally weird!

However, those same people also said that they would happily watch a film like *Armageddon* because they didn't think of it as science fiction.

Investigation

Michael Barry, Marketing Director of the *Sci-Fi Channel*, analysed the results of his audience research and found two types of people and their likes:

- the sci-fi fan who enjoys all the things listed in answers under (a) in the quiz;
- those he called the sci-fi *susceptible*, who enjoy science fiction if it is presented in a way they like, and enjoy all the things in the answers under (b) in the quiz.

Dilemma

How do you keep your hard-core science fiction fan and interest the susceptibles enough to get them into the cinema?

Solution

Include elements of the things that both types like in the narrative, and market the film in a way that appeals to both. Barry came up with the following list of what appeals to both sci-fi fans and sci-fi susceptibles:

- Escapism: immersing yourself in others' lives and actions, forgetting your daily life;
- Fun: entertainment, spectacle, comic moments;
- Having the imagination stimulated: fantastic designs, spectacular action, amazing.

Special FX

- Alternative realities: thinking about life in different ways, different societies, different 'natural' forms;
- High emotion: tension, fear, excitement, thrill, laughter, love - all in a safe environment.

Activity

- Discuss some blockbuster science fiction films that you know and have enjoyed, such as *Independence Day*, *Terminator 1* or *2*, the *Alien* series, *Men in Black*, *The Matrix*, *Mars Attacks!*...
- Choose one and identify what you enjoyed about it. Use the guide which is organised into the different things that 'sci-fi fans' and 'sci-fi susceptibles' enjoy. *Armageddon* is used as an example to start you off.
- Are there also elements in the film you chose, which both fans and susceptibles enjoy?
- After the activity discuss the following question: these films have successfully gained mass appeal, however, what issues do they raise about calling this genre science fiction?

Constructing Science-Fiction Films for Broad Appeal

FILM	Unbelievable/ Believable	Fantasy Reality	Intellect Emotion	Space Earth	Relevance	Broad Themes	Other
Armageddon	Escaping from the exploding Russian space station, training ordinary men to be skilled astronauts in such a short time / *Landing on meteors because we've landed on the Moon and landed vehicles on Mars; drilling the meteor because of the men's oil drilling skills*	Space technology; heroic achievements of the men / *Oil rig; men's weaknesses and self-indulgence*	Discussion of methods to destroy meteor, working out timing / *lovers' poignant parting, horror of Russian trapped in burning space station, sadness of astronaut's death*	Cutting between the people in the space centre on Earth and the action in space	falling in love and possibly losing someone; parents not approving of boyfriend; reassuring - the safe return of the characters we care about	Broad Themes: individual sacrificing himself for the sake of humanity	Entertainment - spectacular action and special effects – great to see in the cinema on a big screen with surround sound; funny - the oil rig chase, Steve Buscemi's character. Great poster image – orange and black fiery image, men look powerful walking towards you

5.6

THE AWFUL TRUTH

What makes a good film poster? As Andrew Pulver finds out, that's the last thing the PR team have to worry about...

A movie poster doesn't just tell you what's on and who's in it — every billboard is an ego-massaging minefield of contractual obligations and legal requirements. Christina Crosse is creative services manager at Buena Vista, distributors of Armageddon, and is responsible for putting together the film's UK poster campaign. As she explains, it's more a case of what you can't leave out than what you're allowed to put in...

1 Bruce Willis

"Bruce Willis has primary position. He's the only one whose name goes higher than everything else. This goes all the way back to when the actors are first signed up and are negotiating their deal — their lawyers and agents all start wrangling over who gets what on the poster. I think Armageddon is still going on. The size of the letters is contractual: they are 20 per cent of the average size of the artwork title — or 100 per cent of the billing block at the bottom."

2 The Head Shots

"If you show Willis, you have to show these two (Liv Tyler and Ben Affleck). If you show those two, you have to show this lot. They all trigger each other. They have to be named as well. You can't show their picture without their names. But you can have their names without their faces.

These are head shots sent from America. There are lots of 35mm stills from the film that we could use but they're not good enough quality to print in a poster because they're so small. These have been retouched in the States, so we're better off using them."

3 The Team Pic

"This evolved as the poster's central image, and it's appeared on all the publicity we've done. It took quite a lot of cracking — it wasn't there when we started."

4 Peter Stormare

"Peter Stormare isn't in that group of head shots; clearly his agent didn't negotiate it. We didn't push for it because even though he's known to the Fargo crowd, he's not going to add anything to sales on this movie. He gets in the billing block, though."

5 The Clinch Shot

"We wanted to bring in the love angle to broaden out the appeal, so that's why we went for Affleck and Tyler kissing. This picture can't be bigger than Bruce Willis opposite because he also controls the size of image. Willis will also have likeness approval. We could pick any shot out to use in the poster, but if he saw it and didn't like it, he could say no. Now, we're supposed to have all the others' pictures in there too and they are — in theory. In fact, this poster isn't a

AUG 1-7 1998

© Andrew Pulver, *The Guardian*

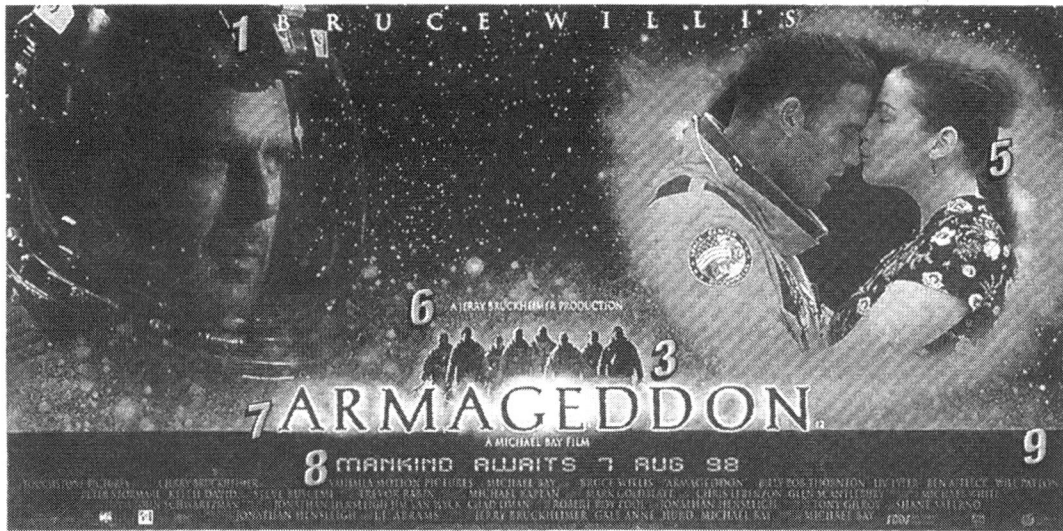

hundred per cent watertight, because you can't really see them clearly in the team pic."

6 Jerry Bruckheimer
"Normally you see the director's name above the title; in this case, the producer has negotiated that he goes above, and the director goes below. The director has equal sizing to Bruckheimer but he's still below him. Don Simpson didn't get that — not on any of the pictures we had, anyway."

7 The Title Block
"We make up a few different logos, using basically the same typeface, but with variations. It's rendered differently on the various posters depending on the background."

8 The Dateline
"The slogan and typeface we came up with ourselves. A lot of the American publicity materials were based on the countdown idea — you know, a countdown to save the planet — and we used this."

9 The Billing Block
"Like the credits, the lawyers all haggled over this right at the start. There's a standard order to it: the production company, then all the cast. The "And" picks out an actor who might not have a huge role but they need to give status to. Then the list of technical credits. It goes in reverse order, with the director going last. The lettering is controlled by the size of the title block — it's normally 25 per cent of the average letter size of the title. We're also contracted to put logos on. We change them if we have to: say we're promoting a soundtrack on a different record label than in America."

The Letter Size
"There has to be a size comparison between all the written credits. The Bruce Willis credit must be 20 per cent of the average size of the letters in the title block — or 100 per cent [the same size] as the billing block. The director and producer credit can't be less than 30 per cent of the billing block."

© *Andrew Pulver, **The Guardian***

The Structure of the Film Industry

The film industry, like many other industries, is divided into three sectors:

PRODUCTION
Making the film

PRE-PRODUCTION

Scriptwriting

Planning e.g. locations, storyboards

Casting

Budgeting
Design e.g. sets, costumes

PRODUCTION
Filming
1st Unit
2nd Unit

POST-PRODUCTION
Editing

Sound Editing*

sound effects**

ADR***

Music soundtrack

*Sound effects and music are recorded separately to ensure greater clarity.

**these include all sounds; human sounds are added by the Foley Artist, named after a sound engineer Jack Foley.

***Automated Dialogue Replacement: actors re-record any dialogue that was unclearduring filming.

DISTRIBUTION
Transporting copies of the film and promoting it to target audiences.

FINANCE
Many companies arrange loans to finance production
Below the line costs
Above the line costs.

PUBLICITY & MARKETING
Advertising
  posters
  trailers
  Publicity
  interviews
  reviews, articles

Promotion
  market research
  previews, premieres
  merchandise
  soundtracks
  web sites

PRINT DEPARTMENT
Makes film and video copies of the film

The amount depends on whether a mass audience or a niche audience has been planned for.

FILM SALES
Book films into cinemas
Sells videos, DVDs to retailers.

EXHIBITION
The film is available for the audience in

Cinemas

Shops

Leisure/entertainment centres

Websites

Making a Pitch and Marketing

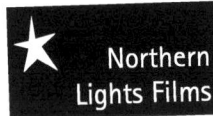

Northern Lights Films

Clerkenwell, London
www.n.lights.com

Dear Blue Moon Production

First let us introduce ourselves. We are an international film distribution company with a commitment to developing new talent in Britain. We want to back a new science fiction film and are inviting producers whose work we like, such as yours, to send us a treatment. We will invite the short-listed selection in to make a pitch and then fund the one which we think will have broad appeal.

Northern Lights works in the small to medium budget range; our first interest is in good stories and characters. We know our audience knows about films, and we need you to use science fiction conventions as interestingly as you can. Here is our brief:

- Have a strong storyline and characters. The treatment should be about 250 words making clear the key information: who, what, where, when and why!
- Have a strong central issue about science and society, particularly one which seems very likely to develop in the 21st century
- Appeal to both males and females
- Reflect modern multicultural life.
- We go for the standard 16–24 target audience age range, but you can convince us to target another good market if you give us the reasons.
- Give us some brief notes on possible casting for the types of characters you want.

We look forward to hearing from you as soon as possible and know you will be original and aware of what is currently getting audiences into cinemas.

Cheers

Evan Mamet

Evan Mamet

Head of Development
Northern Lights Films

Writing Your Own Film Treatment

HELP – I NEED SOME IDEAS TO GET STARTED!

◆ You may already have ideas of your own, so go ahead.

◆ You could research your target audience and find out what they like about science-fiction (and other genres if you want mass appeal).

◆ You may want to make sure that you will satisfy what science-fiction fans expect by using a typical plot.

◆ Look for some ideas about current science and society issues. The basic narrative idea in science fiction comes from the question **What if...?** Science fiction writers start with an aspect of scientific knowledge, or the way the world is now, then develop a plot it by imagining what the issues and consequences might be as the science becomes more sophisticated, or as the world continues in the same way. E.g. what if we created machines that could think for themselves; what if we could clone loved ones who have died; what if we became so over-populated we ran out of food?

HOW DO I TELL THE PLOT?

◆ Check on the notes about how to make film narratives have broad appeal.

◆ Decide on what narrative structure you think will tell the story most effectively, e.g. first person, flashback, recorded evidence, third-person (eye of God).....

◆ Remember that good dramatic stories involve conflict, and often the key issues are: morality, money, power, whose interests are being served.

Remember:

◆ **Plausibility** :It is important for the audience's involvement that they believe, and understand, what is happening on the screen.

◆ **The Present:** Although films might be set in another time, the ideas in them really make the film about the present, it tells us what we imagine, and are concerned about, now – we can't imagine what we can't possibly know.

HOW DO I WRITE THE PLOT?

◆ Discuss your ideas with your partner.

◆ Write a first draft; the important thing is to get your ideas down, so don't worry too much about details at this stage.

◆ Discuss your first draft with your partner. It would also be helpful for your presentation to the distributor if someone who doesn't know about it reads it and offers advice.

◆ Check that you're appealing to your target audience – check the audience research advice.

◆ Check that the genre is clear through using and/or subverting generic conventions

◆ Make notes / annotations on your first draft.

◆ Write a second / final draft.

TYPICAL SCIENCE FICTION PLOTS

There is no fixed way of grouping and describing science fiction plots. However, described for you below are several of what are generally agreed to be the main types of plots:

SPACE FANTASY

This type of plot is set in space and on other planets. The hero usually sets out on an important quest, either alone or with a small group of companions, and has many adventures. It could be a space mission that goes wrong e.g. *Event Horizon, Lost in Space*. There is also a strand called space 'operas' in which the action is large-scale and there is a mythical quality to the characters and story; e.g. *Star Wars* series, *Alien* series.

FUTURISTIC WORLD

These plots show how life on Earth changes as time passes, and the co-existence of life on Earth with other planets. Cities show change more than rural areas so they are more often used. The changes can be through development into a perfect world (utopian), or deteriorate into a bleak despairing world, (dystopian). Both worlds are usually highly mechanised with androids, super-powered vehicles, phenomenal computers, etc. This type of plot is usually a conventional thriller set against the city images; e.g. *Metropolis*, *Blade Runner*, *Escape From New York*, *The Matrix*, *Dark City*, *Robocop*.

ALIEN INTRUSIONS

Earth is threatened or even invaded by an alien force. The normal course of everyday life is disrupted by the (imminent) arrival of intruders from another place or another time. The effect can be destructive, e.g. *The Blob*, *The Thing*, *Invasion of the Body Snatchers*, *Men in Black*, *Mars Attacks!*, *Independence Day*; or benign, e.g. *The Day the Earth Stood Still*, *Close Encounters of the Third Kind*, *Fifth Element*, or accidental, e.g. *E.T.: The Extra-Terrestrial*.

TIME TRAVEL

Characters move backward or forward in time and become involved in changing events. These films often involve complicated plots containing opposing values, clashes of culture, and romances. e.g. *Planet of the Apes*, *Back to the Future* series, *Terminator* series, *Stargate*, *Twelve Monkeys*.

DISASTERS

These can be in many forms – collisions with meteorites, diseases, nuclear wars.
The basic plot follows the attempts of a hero or group to stop the disaster from occurring, or to rebuild life in a new and desolate environment. e.g. *Twelve Monkeys*, *War Games*, *Armageddon, Starship Troopers*.

MENTAL POWERS

These plots centre around humans or aliens who discover, or are discovered to have amazing mental powers. Such characters are often represented as being greatly advanced in brilliance and reasoning, e.g. Mr Spock in *Star Trek*. This power can be used for evil, e.g *The Village of the Damned*, *The Dead Zone*, *Phenomenon*, or for good, e.g. *E.T. : The Extra-Terrestrial*.

BIOLOGICAL SCIENCE / MUTATIONS

Many of these plots are based on, and imaginatively extend, contemporary science. e.g. electricity starting life – *Frankenstein*; men being able to have babies – *Junior*; genetic engineering/DNA – *Jurassic Park, Gattaca*. Scientific discoveries can also be perceived as interfering with Nature and are, therefore, monstrous and destructive, e.g. nuclear radiation in *It Came From Beneath the Sea*, *Godzilla*, *Them* (giant ants).

Ideas From Science and Society

Science ready to let men have babies

by Steve Farrar
and Karen Bayne

BRITAIN'S foremost fertility expert says advances in medical technology mean men can now bear children.

Lord Winston, who as Professor Robert Winston was ennobled three years ago by Tony Blair, says doctors could use today's techniques to implant an embryo in a man's abdomen, allowing him to carry it to term and then have it delivered by caesarean section.

The treatment, overturning millions of years of evolution, would allow homosexual couples to have children and help heterosexuals if the woman could not become pregnant.

It comes as traditional attitudes to parenting are being challenged by the use of in vitro fertilisation techniques, which have helped increasing numbers of lesbians to have children of their own.

"Male pregnancy would certainly be possible and would be the same as when a woman has an ectopic pregnancy — outside the uterus — although to sustain it, you'd have to give the man lots of female hormones," said Winston, who will outline the concept in his new book, The IVF Revolution, to be published in April.

The in vitro fertilisation pioneer, who presented the BBC television series The Human Body, said such foetuses could be implanted inside the man's abdomen with the placenta, through which the baby would receive its nutrients, attached to an internal organ.

Winston, who is head of the fertility clinic at Hammersmith hospital, west London, acknowledged that it would be dangerous as there would be a risk of bleeding from the implanted placenta. In addition, the hormone treatment could lead the man to grow breasts.

Despite this, however, he believed the technique would still appeal to some: "There might be some demand among consenting homosexuals but I don't think there would be a rush of people wanting to implement this technology."

The concept was the central theme of the Hollywood film Junior, in which the unlikely figure of Arnold Schwarzenegger plays a man who becomes pregnant.

Other fertility experts agreed that the fantasy could now become a reality.

Dr Simon Fishel, director of the Centre for Assisted Reproduction in Nottingham, said: "There is no reason why a man could not carry a child. The placenta provides the necessary hormonal conditions, so it doesn't have to be inside a woman."

He revealed that he had been approached in the past two years by three couples who wanted the man to carry the child because of the woman's physical problems. In all the cases he had refused because he felt there were risks.

In one case, the woman had lost her womb as a result of an accident and the man was keen to carry the child rather than involving a surrogate mother.

"They wanted to do it quietly and genuinely," said Fishel. "This kind of treatment is ethically acceptable and one would do it if it could be done without risk."

The procedure's possibilities were recently demonstrated in the remarkable case of a woman in Oxfordshire who carried a baby outside her womb.

A scan revealed the embryo had travelled into the mother's abdomen and had attached itself to her bowel. She decided to continue with this rare type of ectopic pregnancy and the baby was delivered without mishap.

Dr Gillian Lockwood, a clinical research fellow at the John Radcliffe hospital, Oxford, who knew about the case, said: "This shows the possession of a uterus is not absolutely necessary and if this is the case then male pregnancies are theoretically possible."

Although leading figures in the homosexual community predicted that there would be many gay couples keen to carry their own children, any fertility doctor considering it would have to obtain approval from the Human Fertilisation and Embryology Authority.

Suzanne McCarthy, chief executive of the authority, said: "If an application were made, we would give it serious consideration but we would not be interested only in the science of how safe and effective it would be, but also why it was being done."

In western countries women have always played the central role in bringing up children, but attitudes have begun to change. Until the 1960s it was considered unnatural for the father to be present at the birth — today it is the other way around.

Tim Hedgley, chairman of the national fertility association Issue, welcomed the possibility of allowing men to be mothers. "It is not ghoulish in any way and you certainly could not stop a man from doing this in legal terms on the grounds of sex because that would be discrimination," he said.

Some scientists, however, rejected the treatment out of hand. The fact that male pregnancies were possible did not mean they should be allowed, said Ian Craft, an in vitro fertilisation pioneer at the London Fertility Centre. "It would be dangerous and is a distortion of nature," he said.

Among those who would be eager to take advantage of male pregnancy techniques would be homosexual couples, said Mark Watson, a director of the lesbian and gay rights group Stonewall.

"If this option were available, gay couples would certainly take advantage of it as another way of having children," he said.

It would change social attitudes towards parenting and help to convince society that men were as capable of bringing up children as women, said John Baker, a sociologist at the University of Brighton and a member of Families Need Fathers.

"This would remedy an injustice that lies within biology. If a woman wants to get pregnant all she has to do is get a man drunk, while a man has to plead with a woman to have his child," he said.

It was difficult for a man to be an actively involved parent as he was still expected to work long hours, said Dr Jill Dunne, an expert at the Gender Institute in the London School of Economics.

"Before we can even begin to think about whether men can give birth, we have to think of how they can get the time to develop a loving, close relationship with their children," she said.

steve.farrar@sunday-times.co.uk

Arthur C. Clarke, who wrote the book *The Sentinel*, upon which the film *2001: A Space Odyssey* was based, predicted satellite communications. Below you can see examples of some other science fiction ideas which have become reality.

Read through the selection of current issues about science and society to get you started with ideas for your plots. You may find that you use one idea as a central plot, and others could be sub-plots, additional themes or incidents in it.

© *Steve Farrar & Karen Bayne, **The Sunday Times***

© Steve Farrar, *The Sunday Times*

THE INDEPENDENT
Thursday 25 May 2000 ★★★★

HOME NEWS

Gulp! Camera pill takes fantastic voyage for real

BY STEVE CONNOR
Science Editor

MEDICAL SCIENTISTS have boldly gone where no one has gone before; they have recorded a video film of a journey through a person's entire digestive tract.

A pill-sized capsule containing a camera, light and radio transmitter – but no wires – has emulated science fiction by making a "fantastic voyage" from the mouth to the rear end.

In the sci-fi thriller of the same name by Isaac Asimov, made into a film starring Raquel Welch, a submarine and its crew are shrunk and injected into a man's bloodstream. Their mission is to destroy a blood clot in the brain of a man who was the victim of an assassination attempt.

The real-life fantastic voyage was performed on a group of 10 volunteers who each swallowed a torpedo-shaped capsule while wearing a special belt packed with recording equipment, which monitored the capsule's passage through the body.

A joint Anglo-Israeli team, led by Paul Swain, a professor of gastroenterology at the Royal London Hospital, said it was the first time the digestive tract had been monitored with a wireless endoscope. The procedure, described as "pain-

THE TINY TRANSMITTER THAT COULD REVOLUTIONISE TREATMENT

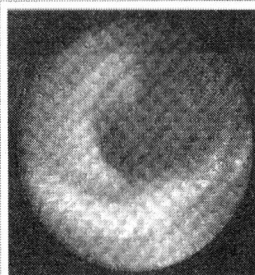

View of the small intestine as transmitted by the camera pill

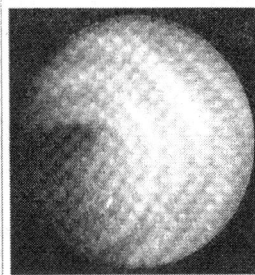

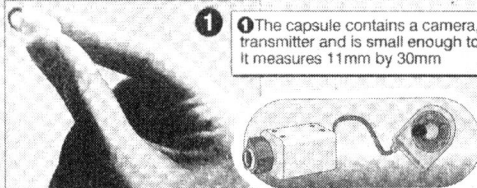

1 The capsule contains a camera, light and radio transmitter and is small enough to be swallowed. It measures 11mm by 30mm

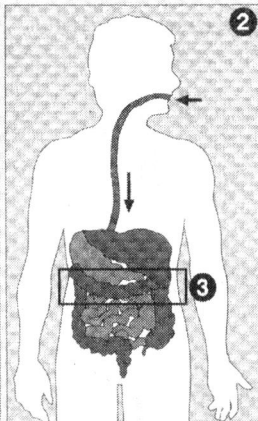

2 The endoscope travels through the stomach and the intestinal tract

3 The video camera inside the capsule sends images to a special belt around the patient's body which contains electronic recording equipment, shown below

4 The capsule takes 24 hours to travel through the gut and is evacuated naturally

less" in the journal *Nature*, involved allowing the capsule to be moved along by the peristaltic contractions of the gut's muscles, until the device was evacuated naturally about 24 hours after it was swallowed.

Video images were transmitted over many hours and collected by the recording equipment on the belt, which also monitored the capsule's precise position in the body.

Professor Swain said one great advantage of the capsule was that it can be used to take images in the small bowel, a region not usually accessible with conventional endoscopses inserted through the rectum.

"I've seen my small bowel and smiled. Not many people can say they've done that because it is usually quite painful in that area," said Professor Swain, who took the capsule.

Another advantage is that patients can undergo endoscopy of the intestines while continuing to carry out their everyday activities.

The capsule measures less than half an inch in width and is just over an inch long. Professor Swain said it was easier to swallow than many antibiotic pills and that patients could not feel it moving inside them.

The scientists, who include electronic engineers from Given Imaging Ltd in Israel, are working on ways of controlling the movements of the capsule so that it can be manipulated near to certain sites of interest within the intestines. One plan is to incorporate a miniaturised cutting device, such as a laser, to take biopsy samples.

Professor Swain said the device had not yet received approval from regulatory bodies in Britain for general use on patients, but he hopes to begin clinical trials this year.

He has not ruled out the possibility of making an even smaller capsule to be injected into the vessels of the blood system – making a real-life *Fantastic Voyage* even more likely.

Leading article,
Review, page 3

© *Steve Connor,* ***The Independent***

Some topical scientific and social issues:

- Who has access to new technologies?
- The hole in the ozone layer
- Voice activated technology
- Global warming
- Natural resources running out
- Surveillance in the streets
- Changing the weather, e.g. creating rain in desert areas
- Religious cults
- Genetically modified food
- Daily extinction of animal and plant species
- Cloning animals and humans
- Human overpopulation
- Widening gaps in society; rich and poor; hi-tech and manual work
- Creating human body parts from human cells
- Insect resistance to pesticides
- Genetic medical treatment
- The changing roles of men and women
- The breakdown of traditional family structures
- Greater longevity
- Recreational drugs
- Cryonics
- Home and personal entertainment, media technology
- International space stations
- Developing understanding of brain power
- Employment in a hi-tech world
- 'Policing' the internet
- Business taking over sport, education and other public services
- Microchip implants into humans
- The spread of advertising and sponsorship: the Mia space station had Coca Cola adverts on it because it needed funding. Also, when a Russian general arrived, he said "I have brought the fruit." Saying this was part of a sponsorship agreement made with a fruit company who were sponsoring the space station.

Research

The website: www.scifimovies.about.com has hotlinks about particular issues which you can access by selecting 'When Science Fiction Becomes Fact' from the menu.

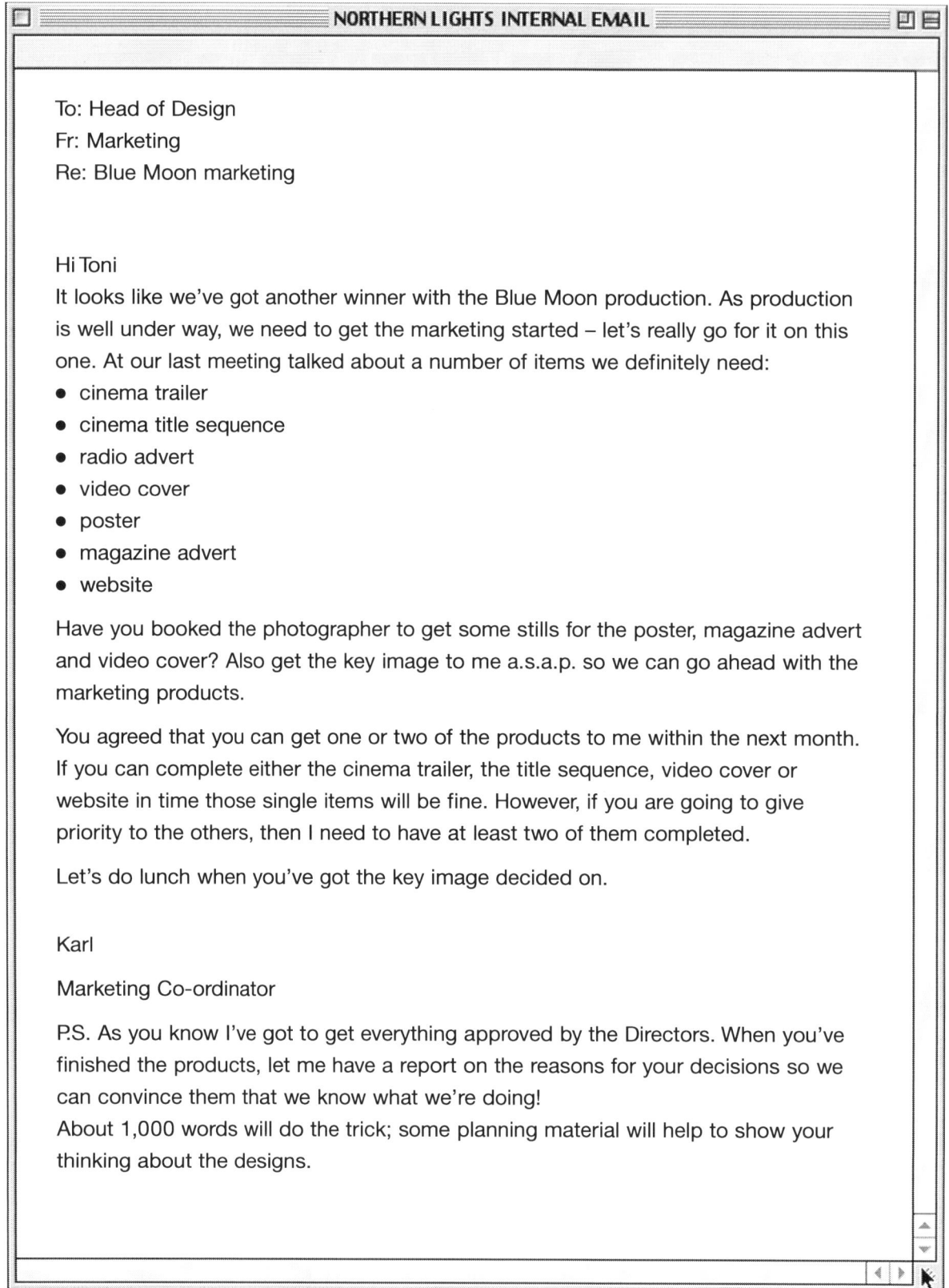

To: Head of Design
Fr: Marketing
Re: Blue Moon marketing

Hi Toni

It looks like we've got another winner with the Blue Moon production. As production is well under way, we need to get the marketing started – let's really go for it on this one. At our last meeting talked about a number of items we definitely need:

- cinema trailer
- cinema title sequence
- radio advert
- video cover
- poster
- magazine advert
- website

Have you booked the photographer to get some stills for the poster, magazine advert and video cover? Also get the key image to me a.s.a.p. so we can go ahead with the marketing products.

You agreed that you can get one or two of the products to me within the next month. If you can complete either the cinema trailer, the title sequence, video cover or website in time those single items will be fine. However, if you are going to give priority to the others, then I need to have at least two of them completed.

Let's do lunch when you've got the key image decided on.

Karl

Marketing Co-ordinator

P.S. As you know I've got to get everything approved by the Directors. When you've finished the products, let me have a report on the reasons for your decisions so we can convince them that we know what we're doing!
About 1,000 words will do the trick; some planning material will help to show your thinking about the designs.

Simulation: Marketing for a Science-Fiction Film

WHO AM I?

You are in role as a member of the design team for an advertising company called CELEBIZZ. Your company specialises in providing marketing and merchandising for forthcoming films.

Your company has just received the following letter offering you a contract with a film distribution company:

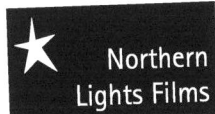

★ Northern
Lights Films

Clerkenwell, London
www.n.lights.com

'Celebizz Inc.'
Covent Garden
London WC2

Dear Sandi and team!

We loved the logo for the T-shirt and felt your bid showed the strongest ideas.
The key image you used was great. We are pleased to offer you the contract to design the pre-release publicity material for our new blockbuster **Moonscape**.

Find attached a brief treatment of the film and a list of your tasks.

All the best

Eduardo Cortex

Eduardo Cortex
Director: Promotions Co-ordination

Treatment:

Moonscape is broadly based on the 'Future Cities' plot, but it also relies heavily on the theme of romance between human and machine. It details the adventures of Carla, a beautiful computer programmer, when she journeys to the moon in 3009. The human colonists had created robots to be their slaves, but she discovers a tiny colony of robots who have altered themselves over the decades to become cyborgs who are almost human in form. Because of her technical knowledge she is able to communicate with them and falls in love with a cyborg called Olivex. Together they try to convince the humans down on Earth that these new creatures are harmless and should be allowed to have their freedom, and to leave the moon and travel to Earth. However, they meet suspicion, danger and attack. In the end, after many adventures, Carla is forced to return to Earth without Olivex.

TASK 1
Storyboard

Design a 10-shot storyboard for a trailer for *Moonscape* that will include the conventions of film trailers. Show the key action, main characters, and hook the audience. Remember that it must be recognisably science-fiction with special effects to match the plot.

TASK 2
Poster

Design a film poster for Moonscape which includes all the conventions of film posters. Remember to choose your key image carefully to suggest something about the plot. Make sure the poster shows that it is a science-fiction film.

TASK 3
Commentary

We would appreciate a short description of your reasons for your design choices for both the storyboard and the poster. This will help a lot when we discuss them at our next marketing meeting. Cheers!

Key words

Simulation:	Working on a task as if it was a real-life situation.
In role:	You become one of the people in the real-life situation, thinking, designing and writing as if you were that person.
Robot:	Moving machine.
Cyborg:	Moving machine that is partly made out of human material.
Conventions:	The way things are usually done so that people easily recognise and understand something.

Reading a Trailer or Title Sequence

Activity

Watch a trailer for a science fiction movie and write about how the audience is enticed into wanting to see it. Use the grid below to make notes.

Denotation: what do you see? (include details)	Connotations: what does it mean?
Titling	The style of the text…
Key Action and movement	The action is… The type of story suggested is… The way the _____ moves…
Key characters	The types of characters are… Their situation seems to be… Their relationship seems to be…
Iconography	The significant objects shown tell us…
Types of shot	The use of CUs…
Colours	The use of…
Matching shots	A smooth sequence of shots is gained by
Pace of Editing	The pace of editing changes…
Voice over, dialogue	The tone of the voice over… The dialogue gives us an idea about…
Music	The atmosphere created by the music…
Mood	The overall mood created is… this fits in with audience expectations about the _____ genre

6.13

© Auteur 2001

Camera shot & angle
Camera Movement
Sound FX
Dialogue/Lyrics
Music
Description of image

Camera shot & angle
Camera Movement
Sound FX
Dialogue/Lyrics
Music
Description of image

Camera shot & angle
Camera Movement
Sound FX
Dialogue/Lyrics
Music
Description of image

Camera shot & angle
Camera Movement
Sound FX
Dialogue/Lyrics
Music
Description of image

Camera shot & angle
Camera Movement
Sound FX
Dialogue/Lyrics
Music
Description of image

Camera shot & angle
Camera Movement
Sound FX
Dialogue/Lyrics
Music
Description of image

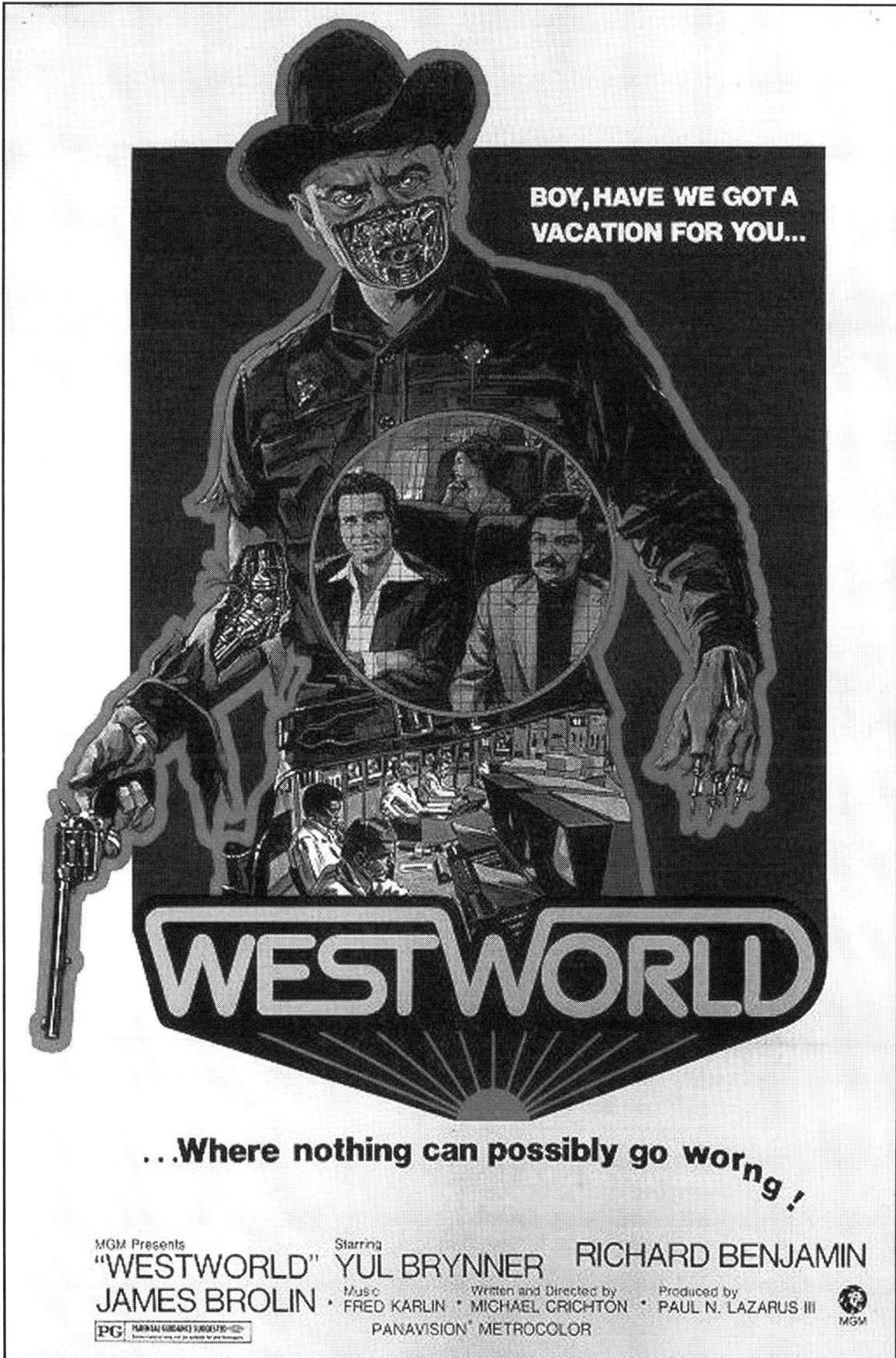

BOY, HAVE WE GOT A
VACATION FOR YOU...

WESTWORLD

...Where nothing can possibly go worng!

MGM Presents
"WESTWORLD" Starring YUL BRYNNER RICHARD BENJAMIN
JAMES BROLIN • Music FRED KARLIN • Written and Directed by MICHAEL CRICHTON • Produced by PAUL N. LAZARUS III
PG PARENTAL GUIDANCE SUGGESTED
PANAVISION® METROCOLOR

Talking and Writing about Film Posters

Activity

◆ Look at the science fiction film poster reproduced here or use your own.

◆ Stick a copy to a large piece of paper. Leave plenty of room around the edges for your notes.

◆ Identify the various parts of the poster, these are listed below in bold, and say what ideas are suggested by them. Go into as much detail as possible.

The parts of a poster:

◆ **Title of the film**

◆ The **font design** (the style of the writing)

◆ The **key image (main picture)**; what ideas does it suggest about the story?

◆ The **tag line**: what does it add to ideas about the story.

◆ The **colours** used and the ideas and mood they suggest.

◆ The **characters**:
  • How many are there? Is there a background that tells you where they are?
  • What type of characters do you think they are, what makes you think this?
  • What can you tell about their situations from their expressions?

◆ The **actors'** names, how are they placed in relation to the title?

◆ **Certification**

◆ Who do you think the **target audience** is?

◆ Anything of interest in the **credits** (usually at the bottom). Who is the producer, the distributor, the director?

◆ Any other **copy (writing)** that tells you something about the film or the people who made it, e.g. reviews, awards...

◆ What **genre** (type) of film do you think it is? Why?

A Frame for Talking/Writing About Posters

The *genre* of the poster is best described as
I know this because

The title of the film is
The title suggests that
The *enigma* posed by the title is
The font of the lettering suggests
The colour of the lettering *signifies*

The main colours are
The design of the *layout* has
The *key image* in the poster is
In the *foreground*
In the *background*
Significant objects include…, suggesting
The main threat in the poster is
The characters in the poster are
The relationship between the characters is *connoted* by
The facial expressions of the characters suggest
The body language is
Their style of dress is
Overall these people appear to be

The star(s) is/ are
The appeal of the star(s) is

The *tagline* suggests
The title and tagline work together to

The film seems to be about
This is denoted by

In the credits the producers and distributors are
The type of production this suggests is

Tie-in products include
The target audience for the film appears to be

The appeal of the poster is

Key Terms

Genre	category or type of film
Enigma	mystery / question / puzzle to solve
Signifies	suggests
Layout	the way in which all the parts are set out
Key image	the main picture (used on all the marketing)
Foreground	near the front of the picture
Background	at the back of the picture
Tagline	a short catchy phrase about the film

© BFI Stills, Posters & Designs

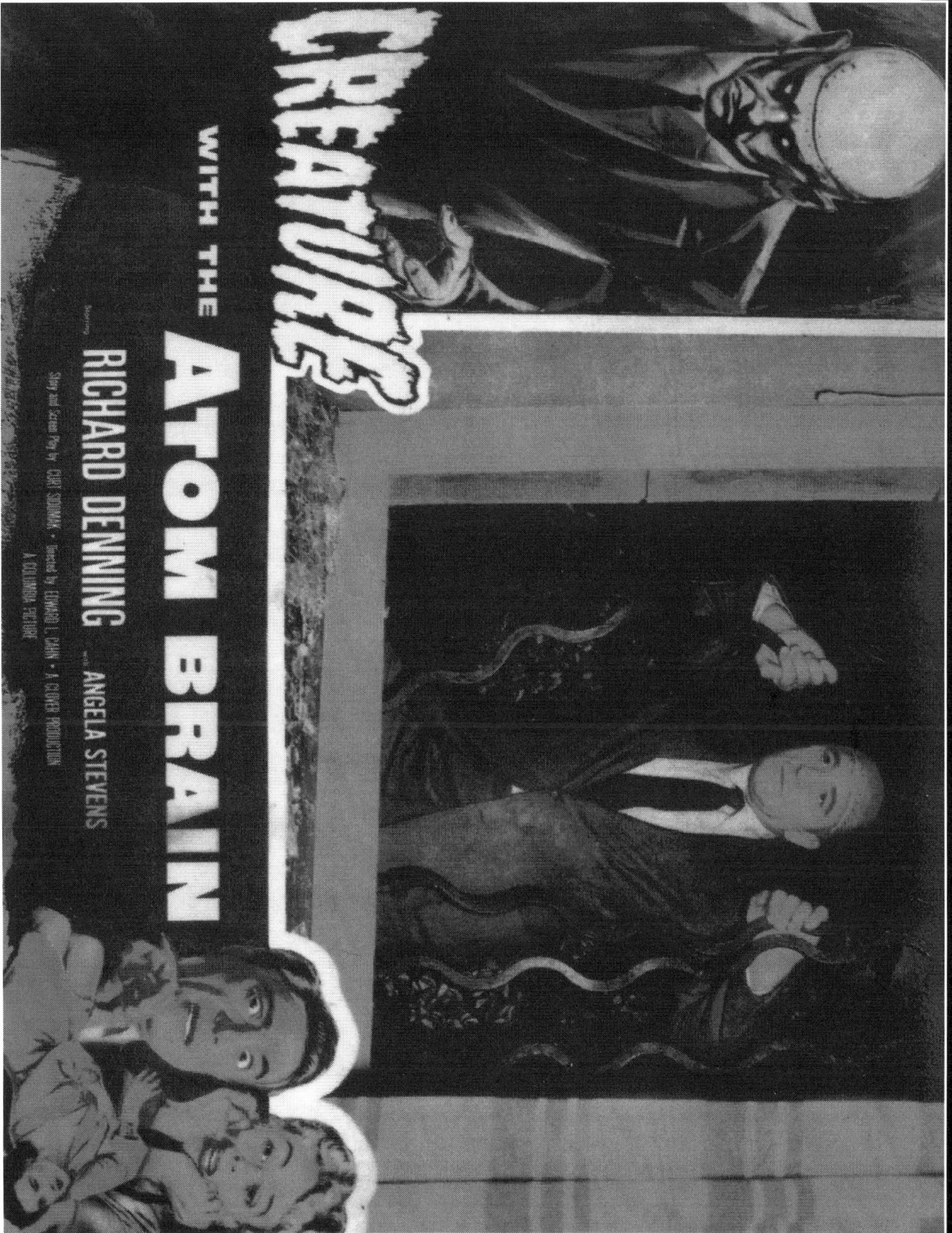

CREATURE WITH THE ATOM BRAIN

Starring RICHARD DENNING with ANGELA STEVENS

Story and Screen Play by CURT SIODMAK · Directed by EDWARD L. CAHN · A CLOVER PRODUCTION

A COLUMBIA PICTURE

Mega Exciting Amazing Film Posters from Outer-Space Featuring Crazy Inter-Galactic Killer-Zombie-Mutant Creatures

The Aims

There are three main aims to this task:

1. To show your understanding of the conventions used in marketing a genre film.

2. To show your understanding of 1950s science fiction film posters in particular.

3. To show some understanding of the main concerns of 1950s films.

Background

In the 1950s a great many small, independent film companies in Europe and America made low-budget genre movies. These could be cheaply rented and would often be exhibited at local cinemas or drive-ins as a double-bill. Science fiction films were a favourite because they were more spectacular (even with obviously cheap special effects) than other double-bill or B-movie genres. The sense of drama and tension was particularly enhanced in America by fears of communist invasion and growing awareness of the destructive effects of nuclear radiation.

In order to encourage audiences into cinemas and drive-ins, more thought was often put into the marketing and publicity for these films than was spent on the production. The poster was a key element in the publicity package. The 1950s were also the time when colour films became established and vivid shades were used to tempt people out of their homes away from their black and white televisions.

TASK

Create a 1950s-style poster. Let your imagination run wild – the 1950s marketing departments did! Also pay particular attention to representation: female characters, the hero, the monster.

Step One
Look at the selection of 1950s posters in detail. Invent a suitable name (or two names if you are prepared to design a double-bill) for a 1950s science-fiction genre movie.

Step Two
Create *splash-lines* (big writing) and write *copy* (small writing, including credits) to go on the poster. These attempt to entice audiences into the cinemas.

Step Three
Draft out a rough version outlining the main visual elements.

Step Four
Choose or design a suitable font for the splash-lines and copy

Step Five
Redraft, by hand or on computer, to make the poster look as spectacular, colourful and dramatic as you can.

Step Six
Write an evaluation using a writing guide if you wish. You should include comparisons with the conventions in the posters you have researched.

© Guild Home Video

Video Cover Activity

- Match the terminology to the parts of the video cover.

- Explain the purpose they have on the cover for the audience.

- Analyse the connotations of the visual images, font designs and content of the copy (writing). i.e., what ideas are being conveyed to the audience?

Terminology:

Film Title

Tag line

Key image (main picture)

Spine title

Blurb / plot synopsis

Reviews

Distributor's logo

Production and distribution credits

Certification

Stills

7.1

E.T.: The Extra-Terrestrial (1982)

✦ Each group can take responsibility for making notes on one of the groups of questions.

✦ You may wish to divide up the questions between you.

✦ Make sure that you provide some evidence from the film, such as dialogue, action, expression, body language, sound, music. Also, visual film language such as camera shots, camera height, camera movement, framing, lighting and shade…

✦ At the end of the film discuss and clarify your notes in your groups – and then feed back to each other in the class so that you each have a full set of notes.

1. Setting

Science-fiction can often be about large-scale settings, imaginary places, have spectacular action and special effects (SFX); heroic or villainous characters:

✦ Where is the film set? How does this affect your engagement with it as a science fiction film?

✦ What are the main groups of people? How are they, and the way they behave, different from what you would expect in a science fiction film?

✦ What representation of adults do we get (e.g. Eliot's mother and father, the teacher, the scientists…)?

2. The relationship between Elliot & E.T.

✦ How are we positioned to identify with E.T. and with Elliott?
How is the developing closeness between Elliott and E.T. shown?

✦ How are Elliott and E.T. feeling at the beginning of the film and why?

✦ Why do you think they become so close? What do they give each other?

✦ What is different about E.T. and Elliott and the way most aliens and humans are represented in science fiction?

3. How are the scientists represented?

◆ What types of shots of the scientists are used, particularly at the beginning? What are we not shown?

◆ Whose point of view (POV) are we positioned to see them from? Who does that positioning make us sympathise with?

◆ What object do you repeatedly see in close-up (CU) on one of the scientists? What ideas does it suggest?

◆ How does the representation of the scientist change later in the film, and why?

4. Science and technology

In science fiction films technology is usually represented as something amazing – either allowing humans to do things beyond their natural capabilities, or alien out of this world equipment to be marvelled at.

◆ Comment on the build-up to the scientists entering and taking over Elliott's home

◆ What are we made to feel about them?

◆ What do you notice about the colours?

◆ What image and colour stand out in contrast?

◆ Compare the alien spaceship to the scientists' equipment

◆ What ideas are suggested about knowledge and understanding?

5. Values

How is a sense of mystery built up around E.T., especially at the beginning of the film?

◆ What other creatures are seen to be sensitive to E.T.?

◆ Why do you think the flower is chosen to represent how E.T. is feeling?

◆ Why do you think the film is set around Halloween?

◆ What part of the body is significant between Elliott and E.T.? What does it represent?

◆ What do you think the rainbow left in the spaceship trail means?

◆ What do you think the film is saying is important in life?

Additional Questions

◆ What references to other films did you notice?

◆ What other stories/genres does the film make you think of?

7.3

TERMINATOR 2: JUDGEMENT DAY (1991) CAN MACHINES BE HEROES AND VILLAINS?

◆ In what ways do 101 and T1000 act like a hero and a villain, or both?

◆ Who else might be considered heroes and villains?

◆ Study the following film extracts to analyse the roles of these two characters in the narrative. The notes in brackets describe the beginning and end of each sequence.

◆ Use the questions to guide your comments, but add anything else you find interesting.

◆ Use evidence to support your points (e.g. action, dialogue, camera work, editing, etc.).

Extract 1: The cyborgs' arrivals

[Lorry radiator grill … end of conversation between T1000 & John Connor's foster parents]

◆ Describe the cyborgs and the first impressions they create.

◆ How is the audience's attitude to them manipulated?

Extract 2: The Galleria – the cyborgs find John

[boys on bike … T1000 walks out of the flames]

◆ How is the view that 101 is malign and T1000 benign continued? E.g., who does T1000 talk to; the appearance of 101, the camera work, etc.

◆ How is the suspense and sense of conflict between the two cyborgs created?

◆ How do you get a sense of the cyborg's strength, speed and non-human qualities?

◆ How does the camera keep the audience near to/amongst the action?

Extract 3: John learns about 101's mission

[101 and John on motorbike … 101 dialogue "…can form solid metal shapes and stabbing weapons"]

◆ What do you learn about 101 and T1000?

◆ How is the pace of editing varied? Describe when and why it is quicker and slower.

Extract 4: John discovers more about 101

[John dialogue "We've got to get her out" … "I order you to help me"]

◆ How does John and 101's relationship change at this point?

◆ What is John shocked by?

Extract 5: Escape from Pescadero State Psychiatric Hospital

[Sarah Connor pinned down … T1000 retrieves his metal]

◆ In what ways are 101's sunglasses significant here?

◆ What more do we learn about the cyborg's abilities?

◆ What sort of 'unit' do Sarah, John and 101 form? How do we now perceive T1000?

Extract 6: Hideout in the garage

[Car enters garage …101 dialogue "No problemo"]

◆ How is 101 made to seem more human?

◆ What role is John developing towards 101?

Extract 7: Battle preparations on the Texas/Mexico border

[John's dialogue "She was with him only one night" … Sarah's voice over (VO) "It was the sanest choice in an insane world"]

◆ What role does Sarah see for 101 and why does it seem like a strangely sane idea?

Extract 8: Sarah finds out about Cybernet and Dyson

[Boys playing with guns … Sarah dialogue "I want to know…everything"]

◆ Compare Sarah's and 101's roles as narrators, e.g. narrative method, what they say, tone of voice, relationship with the audience.

◆ Why does the human race need to be protected from itself?

Extract 9: 101 fends of police at the Cyberdyne Systems building

[Sarah dialogue "Go, I'll finish here" … POV of 101's data]

◆ What is heroic about 101?

◆ What is the moral significance of this scene (refer back to Extract 4)?

Extract 10: Climactic battle at the steel works

[T1000 skewers Sarah's shoulder … light goes out in 101's eyes]

◆ How has the audience's feelings changed towards the cyborgs compared to the beginning of the film?

◆ What other genres of film have this type of 'man'-to-'man' fight?

Extract 11: T1000 is terminated

[T1000, as Sarah, calls John … melted metal]

◆ How is the audience meant to feel about his death?

Extract 12: 101 is terminated

[The microchip is destroyed … POV of 101's data shutting down]

◆ Why does 101 "have to go away"? What does this self-sacrifice make him seem like?

◆ Why does he say to John, "I know now why you cry, but it is something I can never do"?

◆ Why is there an insert of 101 and Sarah shaking hands, and an insert of 101's thumbs up sign? Make connections with previous scenes.

Extract 13: Sarah's final voice over (VO)

[The highway]

◆ What are the connotations of this image?

◆ Is the human race protected from itself?

7.5

TERMINATOR 2: JUDGEMENT DAY (1991)
SARAH CONNOR AND JOHN CONNOR
MOTHER AND SON / HERO AND HERO?

Who is protecting whom?

◆ Study the film extracts to analyse the roles of these two characters in the narrative.

◆ The notes in brackets describe the beginning and end of each sequence.

◆ Use the questions to guide your comments, but also add anything else you find interesting.

◆ Use evidence to support your points (e.g. dialogue, iconography, sound, camera work, etc.).

Extract 1: Introduction of John and Sarah

[Police car computer … John drives off with his friend]

◆ How would you describe John and his 'family' at this point?

◆ How is Sarah first presented to us, and what impression does she make on us?

◆ How and what do we learn about her and how is she regarded by the authorities?

Extract 2: John steals money / Sarah's progress review

[Cash withdrawal screen … dialogue Dr Soberman "…model citizen"]

◆ What more do we learn about John and his attitude to his mother?

◆ What is Sarah so distressed about on the video recording?

◆ What does she seem like on the tape? Comment on the freeze frame.

◆ Why do you think she says she wants to see her son?

◆ Why is the introduction of Dyson edited into this sequence?

◆ Comment on the framing; how are we positioned at the end?

Extract 3: The Galleria – John's first encounter with the two cyborgs

[John and friend play the games machine …escape with 101]

◆ What do you notice about the iconography that is being associated with John? Why is it important?

◆ How does the editing of the cyborgs approaching the arcade illustrate Sarah's fears about John?

Extract 4: John learns about the Terminators' missions / He wants to rescue Sarah

[John dialogue "OK, time out" … "I order you to help me"]

◆ In what ways does John indicate his future leadership qualities?

◆ What do we learn about how Sarah is perceived by others?

Extract 5: Escape from Pescadero State Psychiatric Hospital

[101 and John arrive at the gates... 101 sews Sarah's wound]

- What is significant about the way John is now sitting on the motorbike?
- What do we learn about Sarah's unusual capabilities?
- At what point does she lose control of the situation? Comment on the composition and camera angle when 101 offers her his hand.
- Comment on her actions in the lift.
- What is unexpected about Sarah's behaviour in the car?

Extract 6: Battle preparation at the Texas-Mexico border/Sarah's recurring nightmare

[Sarah dialogue "How much do you know?" ... NO FATE]

- Comment on the way Sarah behaves with the revolutionaries, her clothing and other iconography associated with her.
- Comment on Sarah's voice over (VO). What does the positioning of Sarah, John and 101 during it suggest about how she sees their relationships?
- How is she different from and similar to 101?
- Why do you think we are shown the nightmare at this point rather than when she was talking about it at the hospital?

Extract 7: Sarah at Dyson's home / battle at and escape from Cyberdine Systems

[Sarah walks into the house ... Sarah is wounded in the leg]

- Why can't Sarah kill Dyson?
- What is Sarah's behaviour like compared to the men when they are in the house and when they are at Cyberdine?
- What turning points are there in the relationship between John and Sarah?

Extract 8: Sarah's defiance of T1000 in the steelworks

[John has to leave 101 ... 101 rescues Sarah]

- What are the positive and negative actions of Sarah and John in this sequence?

Extract 9: Sarah terminates 101 / Sarah's final VO

[BCU of John ... John and Sarah watch 101 descend ... dissolve from CU 2-shot of John and Sarah ... black screen]

- What is the significance of the handshake? What has John had to learn?
- What does the composition signify about who is important?
- The VO's have been from Sarah's point of view – however, is she the central hero?

7.7

An Institutional Comparison of a blockbuster movie and a low-budget independent movie

Compare the production values, styles of filming and ideas shown in one of the big budget mainstream films and one of the low-budget, independent sector films described below. Some background information is provided about a choice of two in each sector. You may wish to select other films, and you could also find out additional information through research.

BIG BUDGET MOVIES

Independence Day (1996)

◆ Running time approx. 140 minutes

◆ Produced and distributed by Twentieth Century Fox Film Corporation (TCF)

◆ The Director is Roland Emmerich who previously directed *Stargate* (1994)

◆ **Budget: $75,000,000**

TCF is one of the Big Five major Hollywood studios established in the 1920s which, since the 1950s, has concentrated on producing blockbuster movies and distribution. Like the other major studios, TCF has survived financially by becoming part of a large business conglomerate, in this case owned by Rupert Murdoch's News Corporation. It also owns, amongst many other media, Fox TV and Sky News. TCF recently produced *The X-Files*, and has distributed several other science fiction films including the *Star Wars* and *Alien* series', and *eXistenZ* (1999).

Terminator 2: Judgement Day (1991)

◆ Running time approx. 136 minutes

◆ Produced by Pacific Western in association with Lightstorm Entertainment/James Cameron

◆ Distributed by Carolco

Carolco was a large independent distribution company that specialised in big budget action films. This was a high risk approach which worked very well when the films were successful, but the company no longer exists after having two large scale failures in a row at the box office.

Budget: $100,00,00. A breakdown of costs includes the following (source: *Empire* magazine):

Production costs and special effects	$53 million
Arnold Schwarzenegger's salary	$15 million
(inc. $7m Gulfstream G-111 jet)	
Interest charges to financiers	$10 million
Expenses incurred during production, printing and advertising	$6 million
James Cameron's salary *(for writing and directing)*	$6 million
Payment to Gale Anne Hurd	$5 million
(to buy back the rights to make the sequel to The Terminator*)*	
Payment to Hemdale Films	$5 million
(to buy back the rights to make the sequel to The Terminator*)*	
TOTAL COSTS	**$100 MILLION**

LOW BUDGET MOVIES

Dark Star (1974)

◆ Running time approx. 83 minutes

◆ Producer and Director: John Carpenter; Distributor: Jack H. Harris

◆ **Budget: $60,000**

This was John Carpenter's first feature film, begun during his last year at film school, and taking three years to complete as he tried to raise the money. He went on to make many horror films, including the first *Halloween* (1978), but has stayed mainly in the independent sector. *Dark Star* is a parody of science fiction films.

The Brother from Another Planet (1984)

◆ Running time approx. 108 minutes

◆ Director and scriptwriter: John Sayles, Distributor: A-Train Films

◆ Budget: **c.$200,000**

John Sayles has chosen to work on low budget films in the independent sector because it gives him more freedom to write about the social issues he is interested in, and to explore genre conventions in original ways. One of the ways he gains money to fund his own films is by writing scripts for mainstream films, one of his best known being the horror film *Piranha* (1978). He also likes to work with the same group of actors who enjoy the challenge of varied and complex roles (if you have watched *Terminator 2*, you may recognise Joe Morton who plays the Brother here).

Use the headings that follow below to help you to organise your discussions and writing.

◆ Length of film

◆ Story

◆ Settings

◆ Situations, action

◆ Stars / actors

◆ Characters and how they are represented

◆ Dialogue

◆ Iconography (significant objects)

◆ Themes (ideology); in particular, what ideas, attitudes
  and behaviour are shown to be good or bad?

◆ Technology, special effects

◆ Marketing – if possible

◆ How generic conventions are treated – are they repeated, varied, broken?

◆ Are there any other genres you could use to describe the film?

◆ Evidence of budget, ownership, earning money through advertising
  (e.g. product placement)

7.9

An Exploration of ideology in independence Day (1996)

What do you think is revealed about the values of American society in *Independence Day*?

Discussing ideology involves two main things:

◆ Thinking about ideas. In a film these ideas include what the film suggests is good and something to value and aspire to; and what is seen as bad and, therefore, should be rejected. These ideas relate to our actions, behaviour, beliefs, and attitudes, our personal and public relationships and cultural activities – i.e. the way a society is organised.

◆ Asking questions. How these ideas come about and how they are maintained. Should these beliefs and values be challenged, and how effective are any challenges? Whose interests do these ideas and values serve, and who is kept in power and dis-empowered by them?

Using detail from the text, particularly in relation to the characters, explore how American society is portrayed in the film:

Will Smith	*Capt. Steve Hiller*
Bill Pullman	*President Thomas J. Whitmore*
Mary McDonnell	*Marilyn Whitmore*
Jeff Goldblum	*David Levinson*
Judd Hirsch	*Julius Levinson*
Margaret Colin	*Constance Sparrow*
Randy Quaid	*Russell Casse*
Harvey Fierstein	*Marty Gilbert*
Vivica Fox	*Jasmine Dubrow*
Harry Connick Jr	*Capt. Jimmy Wild (Raven)*

Here are some ideas for you to consider, and to add to if you wish:
◆ Heroism
◆ Families, parenting
◆ A woman's place
◆ America and the rest of the world
◆ Ambition
◆ Religion
◆ Race
◆ Sexuality
◆ Male friendship
◆ Communication
◆ The use of nuclear weapons
◆ Technology

Additional Activity

On the television in Casse's trailer, we are shown a brief clip from a 1951 film called *The Day the Earth Stood Still*. This reference naturally invites comparisons! Using your list as a guide, consider the differences and similarities in the values shown in the earlier film. Can you think of any reasons for these views at the time (i.e. early 1950s)?

Settings: DYSTOPIAN FUTURES

◈ Discuss the ideas about what future society will be like in the three films below.

◈ How does the film language in each film also convey those ideas?
(Film language includes: mise-en-scène, technical codes, genre conventions, narrative structure, etc.)

Metropolis (1926)

◈ Society is led by industrialists and divided into those who live above and below ground.

◈ Suggested Extracts: Cityscape at the beginning and the garden; below ground change of workshifts and entry into the machinery room.

Blade Runner (1982)

◈ In Los Angeles 2019, society is divided into humans who are fit enough to live in off-world colonies, the replicants who service life there, and the less fortunate humans who remain on Earth. Los Angeles is a multi-cultural, predominantly Easternised, industrial city in a post-nuclear winter. (N.B. this last fact is not made explicit in the film, but is the setting for the source book – *Do Androids Dream of Electric Sheep?* by Philip K. Dick).

◈ Extract: Opening sequence up to the end of Deckard's briefing about the escaped replicants.

1984 (1984)

◈ This is a society that keeps everyone under 24-hour surveillance. It is led by the government, under the collective persona of Big Brother. Control is maintained through worship of Big Brother, imprisonment and torture without trial, patriotism through constant world war, and propaganda.

◈ Extract: The opening sequence up to the end of Winston and Parson's conversation at the broken lift about chocolate rations going up.

'A' picture (or 'feature film')	term used during the Hollywood studio period when there were a full length film, double bills and mixed programmes in the cinemas, of which the 'A' picture was the main feature. Given the main budgets and talent
AI (Artificial Intelligence)	the creation of machines that behave in ways which are considered intelligent in human terms – reasoning, speech recognition and reproduction. E.g. computers: HAL-9000 in *2001:A Space Odyssey*; and robots: C3PO, R2D2 in *Star Wars*
American Dream	this represents the inspiration at the core of American society, the **ideology** that the individual is free to pursue and achieve one's ambitions through one's own efforts. It relates to America being a new country to the immigrants who saw the vast land as an opportunity to start a new life free from the restraints many had experienced in their old countries
archetype	the original model, e.g. Ming the Merciless in the 1930s *Flash Gordon* serials formed a model for the appearance and actions of evil characters plotting inter-galactic domination
atomic energy (more exactly termed nuclear energy)	created by neutrons bombarding and splitting uranium or plutonium atoms, this process transforms part of their mass into energy. The energy can be used for a range of purposes including powering domestic fuel stations and making bombs. The issues related to science fiction include the dangers of this phenomenally powerful process and its side effects caused by radiation
audience	as a media concept, 'audience' moves beyond our basic notion of audiences as people who watch, read and listen to the media to an active notion of being crucial in the construction of meaning in the act of 'reading' texts. This active role in the creation of meaning is also seen in the relationship between institution and audience. Audiences' expectations of, uses of, and pleasures in, media texts influence the construction and evolution of individual texts and genres. These audiences are identified by research and categorised in various ways (see **demographic**, **psychographic** and **lifestyle research**). Audiences can also be constructed by producers aiming to create a wish to experience a new media text, or by encouraging audiences to see themselves in particular ways
audience positioning	how producers of a media text guide audience responses; includes the camera position 'placing' the audience in relationship to characters and action on screen
'B' movie/picture	term used during the Hollywood studio era to describe supporting films in a double bill presentation. Shorter, lower budget, using new and fading talents
blockbuster	describes a popular film for which the long queues go around the block and beyond. Now also describes a big budget, high production values, high profit film – usually associated with the 'action' genre but applies to any genre

British Board of Film Classification (BBFC)	the organisation that certifies films and videos according to their suitability for particular age ranges of young people.
capitalism	an ideology based on competition, ownership of property and which aims to maximise the profits of business companies. Also has values associated with individual achievement and freedom for one's actions, for instance associated with the **American Dream**
CinemaScope	Twentieth Century Fox's trade name for **widescreen** filming and exhibition. Most of the major studio had their own versions (and therefore tradenames) of widescreen
Classical or Hollywood Cinema	the form of film developed during the studio era which is now the familiar conventional **mainstream** film
Cold War	the covert conflict following the Second World War until 1989 between the 'free and democratic' West, principally America and western Europe, versus the communist countries, principally Russia and eastern Europe. Symbolised in the alien invasion films of the 1950s and 1960s.
common sense	a phrase used as part of understanding how ideologies work. Unquestioning assumptions made about the world's meanings. The acceptance that the way the world works is obvious and 'natural' and there is no need to challenge it or understand it through considering theories and analysis
communism	the ideology that says property should not be privately owned but shared by the community; individuals should work for the good of the community, contributing according to one's ability and receiving according to one's needs. The positive aspects of its beliefs were undermined through being systematically enforced by fear and violence. America had a particular fear of being invaded by communist countries and their ideology for two main reasons. Firstly communism was in opposition to its own values of capitalism and individualism; secondly many countries near to its borders had become communist – Cuba, Russia (and eastern Europe) China and other countries in the East Pacific such as North Vietnam
Computer Generated Imagery (CGI)	digital special effects
conglomerate	very large company incorporating several different industries, e.g. Time Warner includes Warner films (formerly Warner Bros in the Hollywood studio era), Warner Music and its various 'independent' labels, DC comics; and is merging with AOL digital communications company
context	where audiences consume a media product and how that context affects the meaning of a media product, e.g. if a film is viewed in a cinema, at home, on computer; whether the film is 'made for' cinema, video release, director's cut, etc
construct	a term which foregrounds the fact that all media texts are made through creating, selecting and ordering material

conventions	ways of doing things (constructing films) which are successful, copied by others and, over time, become established. Although sometimes called 'unwritten rules' the word 'rules' is best avoided as it can suggest the slightly misleading sense of prescription and rigidity. Conventions provide the framework for mainstream texts
crossover	media text successful in a different market from which it was originally positioned
cryogenics	branch of physics dealing with phenomena at very low temperatures, popularly associated with 'freezing' bodies for future re-animation
culture	refers to the 'whole way of life' of a society or social groups within a society; more specifically – its beliefs, values, systems of ideas and products
cyborg, or cybernetic organism	the fusion of flesh and machine to form a new and unique being that is almost human; e.g. *Robocop, The Terminator*
demographic research	a method of market research which categorises audiences according to their social characteristics such as social class, age, sex
director	the person responsible for the artistic production of a film or television programme
distribution	the middle stage of the industrial process which has two aspects: firstly, transportation of products to their places of sale (exhibition); secondly, marketing to raise awareness of new products. (Also see **production** and **exhibition**)
dystopia	science fiction term describing a society which is horrific; usually set in the future showing how our present society may deteriorate
ego	according to Freudian psychology, the rational socially responsible part of the human personality which also controls the impulsive 'id'; the 'I' or self which is conscious and thinks. (Also see **id**)
eugenics	the science of human race improvement 'improvement' of human races by selective reproduction and other social practices
exhibition	the final stage of the industrial process where the product is displayed for sale; i.e. the cinema, video shop, etc. (Also see **production** and **distribution**)
event movie	usually a big budget blockbuster accompanied by lots of publicity, e.g. *Star Wars: Episode 1 The Phantom Menace*
feminism	an ideology advocating the rights of women to have equal status and opportunities as those possible for men
gene line engineering	treating human's reproductive cells so that genetic modifications are passed on to children. Could eliminate inherited diseases, could have unforeseen side effects. Currently illegal
gene therapy	'good' genes are placed into the bodies of people suffering from genetic diseases. This treatment affects only the individual treated
general release	the exhibition of a film in cinemas across the whole country; also known as 'blanket release'

genetic modification	changing the genetic make up of organisms to achieve supposed improvements in farming. As well as crops, research is turning to animals, e.g. farmed salmon which can grow four times faster than wild salmon
genre	commonly used as a term to categorise the narrative and style of texts. Media Studies questions the limits of this way of thinking about genre by exploring other ways to group films – for instance by considering the roles of **audience** and **institution**
Hollywood studio system	the organisation of the American film industry c.1929-1960 during which film production, distribution and, until 1948, exhibition were dominated by about 8 major studios and their working practices
hybrid genre	term used to describe a film text which has roughly equal mixtures of different narrative styles, e.g. *Frankenstein* (science fiction horror); *The Terminator* (action, thriller, science fiction); *Men in Black* (comedy science fiction).
icons	originally Eastern European paintings of the Christian God, Jesus and the saints, used as objects of worship. Now the term is also applied to describe images of **stars** in the media and cultural objects which have made a powerful impact and appear in many other contexts from their original ones. The images effectively achieve almost a god-like status. E.g. Frankenstein's monster; Arnold Schwarzenegger and Linda Hamilton in *Terminator 2*; *Judgment Day*; the robot in *Metropolis*
iconography	a term from Art History and Film Studies; it is a collective term used to describe the familiar images in a genre, e.g. spaceships, futuristic cities, tight-fitting costumes in science fiction films
id	according to Freudian psychology, the 'raw' part of the human personality comprising powerful instinctive forces for pleasure and pain. (Also see **ego**). E.g., Dr. Morbius in *Forbidden Planet*
identification	the process by which audiences empathise with and take viewpoints about, narratives, ideas and characters in texts. Most commonly this means identifying with the hero
ideology	sets of ideas or beliefs about the world, which in reality present only selective or partial understandings. How these ideas are related to power in society, i.e. whose interests they serve, and how those ideas seem 'natural'.
independents	organisations in the production, distribution and exhibition sectors which are usually not controlled by large media organisations. They may be owned by larger organisations, but are valued for their more daring and innovative natures
institution	the organisations which produce, distribute and exhibit media texts. Their working practices, technologies and regulation are evident in the media texts they produce. Institutions are also part of and, therefore, reflect broader social, cultural, economic, political and historical contexts. Institution thus also means cultural values

intertextuality	film-makers add meanings to their media texts by direct and indirect references to other media texts, e.g. *Galaxy Quest* is an indirect parody of *Star Trek*; a direct reference is made in made in *Independence Day* in which a scene from *The Day the Earth Stood Still* is seen on a television set
key image	in film marketing the visual image that encapsulates a film's narrative and style; used in all of the marketing and advertising products, e.g. the five elipses of *The Fifth Element*; the black-garbed dynamic stance of Keanu Reeves in *The Matrix*
lifestyle research	a method of market research which classifies audiences according to how they spend their time and money
mainstream	often associated with mass markets; products which are conventional, unadventurous in style and form, and express dominant cultural values
majors	large and powerful organisations which dominate production, e.g. the Hollywood film studios
market	the potential and actual producers and buyers for products
marketing	the process of making potential buyers aware of a product
mass (audience, market and media texts)	texts designed to appeal to the widest possible audience
media language	the ways media texts communicate with the audience; their forms and conventions
mise-en-scène	French term related to theatre referring to everything that can be seen on the stage (literal meaning: putting the scene together). Everything seen in the film frame – setting (time and place), props, lighting, characters, costume, colour design, camera work…
mode of address	how a text speaks (through written, sound and visual language) to its audience thus creating particular relationships between producers and audiences
morphing	the computer generated process of changing smoothly from one shape to another, e.g. the T1000 Terminator in *Terminator 2: Judgment Day*
nanotechnology	the engineering of the very small, e.g. molecule-sized machines. The science fiction issue is that they will be likely to reproduce themselves from raw material
narrative	the organisation of fiction and non-fiction texts; the way a story is told
niche (audience, market and media texts)	texts designed to appeal to a small and/or specialist audience in a segment of the market
persona	originally the masks worn by actors to represent character types in Roman drama. The constructed image of a media star via the roles they play and the publicity about them
pitch	to try to persuade someone to give you the means to make your film

plot	the events of a story with the additional element of character motives, e.g. Sarah Connor ran from T100 because she thought he had returned to kill her (however, can be used interchangeably with 'story')
post-production	editing and sound dubbing after the principal photography stage of production
pre-production	the preparation stage of filming involving, for example, detailed designing and planning, storyboarding and set construction
producers	a broad term used for the organisations, artists, crew and managerial staff who make media texts. Also used more specifically in relation to film for the key person behind the organisation of a film; his/her input can vary from providing facilities, raising money, making vital contacts to facilitate production, to artistic input
production	the first stage of the industrial process in which a media text is made. (Also see **distribution** and **exhibition**)
production values	the amount of money spent on production; audiences can see from what is on the screen whether a film is low budget or high budget
psychographic research	a method of market research in which audiences are categorised into personality types
repetition and variation	the pattern of familiar and new conventional styles in a genre, the mixture aims to reassure and stimulate audiences
representation	the messages conveyed by the way the media presents events, people, places and issues
robot	a machine with artifical 'human' intelligence, usually constructed to look like a form that humans feel they can have a relationship with, e.g. human, animal
science fiction	narratives employing the imaginative projection of how societies have developed and may develop, particularly as a result of technological capabilities
sci-fi	often used as an abbreviation of science fiction; a term of criticism used by serious science fiction enthusiasts about the superficial fantasies which claim to be science fiction
serials	short films with continuous plots, made during the **Hollywood studio** era in which each episode ended on a cliff hanger, e.g. *Zorro*
series	short films in film programmes during the **Hollywood studio** era in which each episode was a complete narrative, e.g. *Flash Gordon*
S.E.T.I. (Search for Extra-Terrestrial Intelligence Institute)	an official organisation, seen in *Independence Day*, which searches radio waves for signs of extra-terrestrial life
SFX	Special effects used to create visual illusions

soundtrack	the overall audio part of a text – dialogue, music and sound effects
splash lines	otherwise known as **taglines** (see below); splashlines can be more prominent in style
star	popularly perceived as an actor with special 'magical' qualities. In Media Studies also an actor whose image is enhanced by careful publicity; able to attract **audiences** and be a selling point for a film
stereotypes	categorisation of people into oversimplified representations; can be negative or positive
story	the events of a narrative's **plot**, e.g. Sarah Connor ran from the Terminator (however, it can be used interchangeably with plot)
structuralism	theories which propose that underlying rules or structures are common to apparently different texts and produce similar meanings
sub-genre	a **genre** within a gonrc; a particular group of films which have more in common with each other than the rest of the film texts in the same genre, e.g. space adventures in science fiction
sync	an abbreviation of 'synchronisation'. Sound and visual images match in time
taglines	otherwise known as slogans in advertising; brief catchy phrases in film marketing products that summarise or suggest the narrative of a film
talent	artistes, performers
target audiences	the specific audiences for whom media texts are designed and marketed
Technicolor	colour film developed in the 1930s but not fully invested in until the 1950s as part of the tactics to win back audiences to the cinema. Often associated with rich vibrant shades of colour
tie-ins	wide range of products made to publicise a film
trailer	a short film, 15 seconds to about 3 minutes depending on the exhibition context, shows key characters and narrative moments to interest a potential audience
treatment	the outline plans for a film which gives a plot outline, genre, suggestions for casting, locations, rough budget; it can also be a preliminary script
utopia	an ideal society (opposite of **dystopia**)
virtual reality	computer simulations representing real things
widescreen	screen ratio in which the width is markedly greater than the height of the screen (16:9)
xenotransplantation	uses organs from specially bred animals, usually pigs, to transplant into human beings

big close-up (BCU)	camera shot in which the face fills the screen
close-up (CU)	head and shoulders camera shot
continuity	matching of details within shots
continuity editing	the matching of action from shot to shot, and matching choices of shots e.g. a series of **CUs** during a conversation with one character looking left, and the other looking right so that they seem to be looking at each other. The aim is for a 'seamless' flow of action so the audience does not notice the cuts
crane shot	a shot from high above with the camera mounted on a crane
crash edit	**editing** using two domestic video machines
cross-cutting / intercutting	editing which cuts between two lines of narrative that are happening at the same time, this is an effective device to build tension
cue	to set up a film or audio tape at the point to begin recording or transmission
cut	an edit which switches from one **frame** to the next
cut-away	a shot or **sequence** of shots placed in a scene that shows separate but relevant action elsewhere
dialogue	the words spoken by the characters
dissolve	an edit in which the final image in a sequence fades and overlaps with the image which begins the next sequence
dolly	a wheel (and trolley) for a camera to be mounted on and moved around
editing	selecting **sequences** from **footage** and putting them in narrative order
editing in camera	shooting action in the order of the narrative
establishing shot	usually a **VLS** at the beginning of a scene which places characters in a location; keeps the audience clear about where they are
exposure	the amount of light entering a camera, controlled by the iris
fade	an edit in which the final shot in a **sequence** fades to a blank screen
fade up	an image gradually emerges from a blank screen
focus	the part of the camera adjusted to keep images clear (sharp focus) or, if required for a particular mood or narrative purpose, to make images a little hazy by being slightly out of focus (soft focus)
footage	the film or video tape that has been shot; also the actual length of film shot
frame	a single shot; also what is chosen to be placed within the four sides of the camera frame
freeze-frame	the action of a film is stopped to capture a single frame image

hand-held	the camera is not on a tripod; hand held cameras are often used as a convention to suggest reality because of its characteristic jerkiness of movement
high angle	shot taken from above
insert	a shot added into a sequence that gives information to the audience, e.g. **CU** of a significant object, a character's reaction to which the other characters are unaware
jump cut	**editing** in which the **cut** is deliberately noticeable
key light	the main lighting for a scene; this can be high (bright) or low (shaded)
log sheet	list of shots completed in order of shooting to be selected and reorganised for **editing**
long shot (LS)	complete body shot in which some of the characters surroundings arc also shown; also, very long shot (VLS)
low angle	shot taken from below
medium close up (MCU)	shot of characters from chest upwards; often used in a **two shot**
medium shot (MS)	shot of characters from the middle upwards
montage editing	visual images are placed in **sequence** (juxtaposed) to create meaning; the **cuts** from shot to shot are often noticeable. A contrasting style of **editing** to continuity editing
music / soundtrack	this can be specially composed or existing music may be used in the background to create moods appropriate to the action. If composed for the film it often includes themes associated with each of the main characters or groups of characters
off-line editing	the rough edit usually done on sub-broadcast level tape
on-line editing	the final edit done on broadcast quality tape
over-the-shoulder shot (OTS)	the camera is positioned behind a character so the audience sees the action over his/her shoulder. Often used during conversations or to create a sense of surveillance
pan	the camera is kept in one place and turns sideways right or left, e.g. to survey a scene. As a rule it goes no more than a semi-circle (180 degrees) otherwise the audience might become disorientated. Going past 180 degrees is known as 'crossing the line'
point of view shot (POV)	the camera is positioned as a character and the audience sees the action through that character's eyes
pull back	the camera moves from CU to LS
reaction shot	shows a character's response to a piece of action or dialogue
sequence	series of shots of a segment of action
sound effects	popularly used to mean sounds artificially created for special effects. In media terms - all sounds in a media text apart from dialogue and music. Usually added on in the post-production stage

split screen	two or more images are shown on the screen at the same time
still	a static image
steadicam	a camera attached to a series of joints and mounted on a body harness worn by a cameraperson; this allows for smooth **hand-held** camera work which can follow action and get close into it
storyboard	a visual plan of how a **sequence** will look; also includes instructions for sound, camera movement, how long a shot will last, notes on action and dialogue.
tilt	the camera is kept in one place and moves up and down
track	the camera keeps alongside a moving piece of action; it is usually on a **dolly** moving along narrow 'railway' tracks
two shot	two people are shown in the **frame** together so the audience know who is talking with whom; can be at the beginning of a conversation and known as an establishing two shot
voice over (VO)	voice outside the film action that explains, gives a personal view about the action
wipe	an edit where one image moves across the screen followed immediately by the next one
zoom	a mechanism on the camera which moves the shot from LS to CU

Other recommended glossaries for technical terms

Storyboards, Film Education
A comprehensive account, with some illustrations, of the key terms and techniques that pupils are likely to use in their practical coursework. Explained in accessible English for most abilities.

Film Art: An Introduction, Bordwell & Thompson, McGraw Hill 5th ed. (1997), pp.477-482.
Detailed and comprehensive catalogue suitable for advanced levels, and a valuable teacher's resource.

Contact details and address are given at the end of this section.

CASE STUDIES OF FILMS

Independence Day,

* *Study Guide*, Film Education: guided case study of the posters and trailers.
* 'Making a Movie and Making Money: Independence Day', BFI Mediawatch Special 1995, pp.12-13: article about the film's financial, production and marketing contexts.
* 'The Evil Has Landed', *Time Out* 24/7/96, pp.18-20: discussion of generic and historical context.

Judge Dredd

* *Study Guide*, Film Education: film and comic conventions and the marketing campaign.

Frankenstein

* *Kenneth Branagh's Frankenstein* Pan (Macmillan), 1994: production background, film script extensively illustrated with stills.

Jurassic Park

* *The Making of Jurassic Park*, J. Duncan, Boxtree Ltd, 1993: production information.

Men in Black

* *Men in Black*, ed. Sonnenfeld, Solomon, Parker & MacDonald, Penguin, 1997: script, stills and story behind the film.
* *Study Guide*, Film Education: includes cross-genre and historical context.

Stargate

* *Study Guide*, Film Education: includes activities exploring the concept of genre.

FILM TEXTS

Many good video shops and local libraries have good ranges of science fiction films for hire, including past 'classics' such as *Frankenstein*, and 1950s films which have been re-mastered and re-released. Other good sources include:

* **BFI video** catalogue, tel. 020 7957 8960; email: marketing.films@bfi.org.uk. On-line catalogue: www.bfi.org.uk/bookvid/videos/indexphp3
* **Movie Mail:** www.moviem.co.uk
* **Black Star:** www.blackstar.co.uk

FILM LANGUAGE AND PRACTICAL WORK

DVD formats of individual texts often have extensive additional material such as 'the making of' the film, including a commentary by directors, designers and cinematographers about the filming choices and technology. Other supplementary material useful for discussion includes deleted scenes, alternative endings and picture galleries. Occasionally marketing campaigns are documented, for example providing several trial versions and the published version of a film's poster, and are particularly useful for foregrounding the process of planning to pupils. You may find the following useful:

* *Backtracks*, BFI: CD-rom activities focusing on the relationship between sound and moving image.
* *Film Language*, Film Education: includes video of film extracts for detailed analysis. Booklet includes explanations of film language conventions, analytical and creative exercises, models of analytical film writing, illustrations from a wide range of classic and modern texts.
* *Moving Images in the Classroom*, BFI/English & Media Centre/Film Education. Aimed at KS3 and cross-curricular study; however, chapter 1 provides a rigorous, focused model of teaching and reading film techniques. Available free from BFI Education Projects (The Guide), 21 Stephen Street, London W1T 1LN; email: alpa.patel@bfi.org.uk.
* *Picture Power* booklet and CD-rom, English & Media Centre. A hands on introduction to image analysis, narrative construction and genre; good starting point for learning the skills of practical production.
* *The Storyboard*, Film Education: explains how storyboards are used professionally; provides an example and a glossary of filming terms.

FILM MARKETING AND AUDIENCES

Academic Resources

* *Film and Audience*, Film Education
* *The Film Industry Pack*, Film Education: Comprehensive information in 5 study guides which explain and illustrate, with related student activities, the processes of the three industrial sectors: Production, Distribution and Exhibition. An excellent resource, particularly the marketing section, including case studies, documents, and video compilation of trailers.
* *Marketing: Media Studies Guide*, BFI.
* *The Marketing of a Film: Judge Dredd – A Case Study*, BBC2. Useful discussion of key image construction and audience targeting. Also see Film Education booklet above.
* Textual Resources (also Websites below)

Magazine adverts

Film and lifestyle magazines obviously carry adverts, but the following are particularly recommended for carrying several to choose from:

* *Empire*, film magazine: DVD and video version adverts.
* *Q*, music magazine with substantial film section.
* *Time Out*, listings magazine: has a good range of film advert styles.

Posters

Apart from buying posters from high street stores and cinema foyers, you can get free samples from video shops and film fairs. Cinemas are another source, and some managers will kindly send you the press kits they receive. Journalists are recipients of many press kits, though it may be more diplomatic to contact your local newspaper than the national papers and magazines.

* **BFI Stills, Posters and Designs Section**, tel. 020 7957 4797. They will do a search of their transparencies collection for what you want in response to your telephone call, then you have to write/fax/email a written request for a hard copy. They provide laser copies of full size posters or multiple smaller prints; cost depends upon the nature of the requesting organisation and usage of the posters.
* **Flashbacks**, tel. 020 7439 8525
* **The Movie Posters Archive** http://anubis.science.unitn.it/services/movies has contemporary examples and a good selection of 1950s posters; click on blue circles for alphabetical examples of contemporary posters.
* **6 Degrees** www.6degrees.co.uk/en/2/200006ftsciencefictionpast (and present.html)
* **Vintage Magazine Company** (film posters, memorabilia, magazines), tel. 020 7437 8562

Trailers

Hired video cassettes have full length trailers before the main feature; if you are lucky to have a local library that rents out videos, the fee is much cheaper than a shop and you can often keep them for a week.

* *Empire:* occasional free CD-rom collections, also available from back copies
* Film Education: video and CD-rom collections
* *Teaching Trailers*, Film Education: downloadable student study material via their website: www.filmeducation.org

Additional Websites

Film posters and video covers give their individual film websites, though these can be short-lived. The addresses noted below are highly selective for the sake of brevity. If you want a more comprehensive choice or to browse for yourself, then the search engine Google is fast and comprehensive in its response to a search phrase such as 'science fiction film posters' or 'science fiction film trailers.'

* **www.apple.com/trailers/** These are mostly current and useful for studying different generic styles and narrative structure. The studio hotlinks contain recent examples that often include science fiction trailers.

* **www.imdb.com** Internet Movie Database. A good starting point as it has about 150,000 texts on file. Information includes synopses of a vast range of films, casts, crews, facts, production news, new releases, reviews, multi-media links and hotlinks to official film sites. Tends to concentrate on recent films; also check plot synopses as they are not always accurate – especially for 'classic' films.

* **www.scifimovies.about.com** The key science fiction film site; has hotlinks to individual film sites via alphabetical list on the left of the home page.

* **www.yahoo.com/Entertainment/Movies_and_Films/** Has an A-Z index of about 10,000 film-related links; very good range of information including financial performance, reviews, and theory.

ORGANISATIONS AND SOURCES OF INFORMATION

The two following publications are published annually, with comprehensive lists of all the current UK media production companies, organisations and facilities. The marketing companies will sometimes give free samples of their posters.

* The BFI Film and Television Handbook (published annually in November)
* The Media Guide, (The Guardian, JEM Marketing, Little Mead, Cranleigh, Surrey GU6 8ND

* BFI Library Information Service, tel. 020 7255 1444; email: library@bfi.org.uk Always reliably informative and helpful.
* *Mediawatch*, occasional BFI/Sight and Sound supplements which provide institutional, economic and audience information about the film market, and UK television. Former versions of the supplement have been the British Film Institute Special (1995) and Media Studies Special (1996-98).

Monthly Film Magazines
* *Sight and Sound*, BFI: the most informed and scholarly magazine; includes full credits for current month's releases with a comprehensive synopses and considered reviews. Supplementary annual Index lists previous year's reviews, and articles in the main body of the magazine. Subscriptions Dept. (code4016), Sight and Sound, Tower House, Sovereign Park, Market Harborough, Leicester LE16 9EF; or www.magazineshop.co.uk or www.bfi.org.uk

* *Empire*: top-selling film review magazine aimed at a predominantly male cinema-going audience, 17-24 age-group with designated hip style. More gossipy and superficial than it used to be, but has succinct reliable reviews, box-office information, and articles about current productions and popular actors.

* *Hot Dog*: launched in 2000 also aimed at a hip young market but for those with a more 'serious' interest in films as, apart from current reviews, it includes detailed coverage of classic films, actors' careers and historical articles.

* *Screen International*: the industry magazine but very useful for production information.

* *SFX*: best-selling of the specialist science fiction and fantasy film magazines, informed coverage of films and other science fiction media texts. Other notable magazine titles include *Dreamwatch* and *Starlog*.

Distribution Companies/Contact Addresses for Educational Materials
* BFI Publishing (unless otherwise stated): Plymbridge Distributors Ltd, Estover Road, Plymouth PL6 7PZ

* English & Media Centre: NATE, 50 Broadfield Road, Sheffield S8 0XJ

* Film Education: Alhambra House, Classroom Resources, 27-31 Charing Cross Road, London WC2H 0AU. E-mail guideorders@filmeducation.org
Website: http://www.filmeducation.org   Tel: 020 7976 2291